The **Politically Incorrect Guide™ to**
the Middle East

The Politically Incorrect Guide™ to
the Middle East

Martin Sieff

Since 1947
REGNERY
PUBLISHING, INC.
An Eagle Publishing Company • Washington, DC

Cataloging-in-Publication data on file with the Library of Congress

ISBN 978-1-59698-051-8

Published in the United States by

Regnery Publishing, Inc.

One Massachusetts Avenue, NW

Washington, DC 20001

www.regnery.com

Manufactured in the United States of America

10   9   8   7   6   5   4   3   2   1

Books are available in quantity for promotional or premium use. Write to Director of Special Sales, Regnery Publishing, Inc., One Massachusetts Avenue NW, Washington, DC 20001, for information on discounts and terms or call (202) 216-0600.

To Debbie Yavelak Sieff

My beloved wife, inspiration, and life partner
who was with me every step of the way, as always.
Thank you, darling.

CONTENTS

Contents

Contents

REVEALING THE TRUTH ABOUT THE WORLD'S MOST POLITICALLY INCORRECT REGION

T he Middle East is the antithesis of every liberal fantasy. And yet probably no region in the world, not even Africa, is so chock-full of virulent, politically correct mythology, distortions, and cover-ups that combine religion, race, the Cold War, America's enemies, and a history of colonialism.

It's a tricky walk for the mainstream media and Ivy League academics, but somehow they manage to paint religious fundamentalists (the Left's usual enemies) as the victims, and the region's tiny religious minority (Israel's Jewish population) as the oppressors. As always, America is the bad guy, and the terrorists are just desperate freedom fighters. If terrorism and Islamic extremism are a problem, the establishment tells us, it's all part of a millennia-old dispute in which both sides are to blame. And, of course, it's rooted in that source of all ills: religion.

While the purveyors of political correctness about the Middle East may not be consistent in their arguments, they are at least persistent in their central theme: America and Israel are bad.

Political correctness has also visibly seeped into some minds on the American Right—most notably in the administration of George W. Bush— who, so ready to buy into the egalitarian PC myths we are all taught, believed that Western-style democracy could flourish anywhere, even in the Middle East. This was to shortchange what an accomplishment

1

Western democracy really is. It fails to realize how hard it is to transplant democracy into a region that has, by and large, rejected not only democracy's Judeo-Christian foundations (Japan managed to do that), the extraordinary cultural contributions of ancient Greece and Rome (Japan managed to do that too), but even the very English system of law and government. This system is the fullest expression of modern democracy and was the system of the Middle East's one-time—albeit short-time—colonial master.

In the Middle East, the cost of PC distortions can be measured in the lives of American soldiers, Iranian dissidents, and Israeli Jews. Pretending there's some sort of moral equivalence between Israeli missile strikes and Palestinian suicide bombers, acting as if our current war is against "terror" rather than against radical Islam, believing that what might have been a militarily sound policy at one time (toppling Saddam during the first Gulf War when we had the troops in place to do the job thoroughly) would still be a good idea ten years later (on the cheap, with a light force, and wedded to a foreign policy of global democracy)—all of these PC delusions weaken the U.S. policy in the Middle East.

In this book, my goal has not been to turn out an academic treatise on the history, culture, and religions of the Middle East. Rather, it has been to reveal the harsh facts about a violent and important region of the world. This book is written as myth-buster. It injects a harsh dose of what Harry Truman called "Plain Speaking" into a public debate that has been fogged over by the endless noble-sounding lies of media elites and foreign policy experts.

What works, and what doesn't

Peace and stability in the Middle East are crucial to American security and the world's economy, and so we all need to shed our PC filters to see what has worked in the past and the present to bring calm and order. The answer is not a feel-good canard like "addressing the root causes of terrorism," or an idealistic dream like democracy in a region where that has never worked outside the confines of Israel and the military state of Turkey. The answer lies in recognizing the inherently, violently tribal culture of the Islamic Middle East, which is the enemy of all order—unless it is imposed from above with a mailed fist. For centuries that fist belonged to the Ottoman Empire.

Today, it is crucial for our own interests that the mailed fist come not from fundamentalist Iran, and not from us (we haven't the resources or the will to do it), and not from Israel (which cannot do it), but—wait for it—from Michael Moore's villain, Saudi Arabia. The Saudis are incompetent at their own public relations in the West, but they are the one generally pro-Western regime in the region that can realistically bring stability and suppress the naturally chaotic peoples of the desert, thanks to their wealth, prestige, and ownership of the holiest places in Islam. The Saudis are also America's longest standing ally in the region—even longer than Israel. Their harsh, underreported crackdown on terrorism in recent years—and their desire for a functioning oil economy—make them the perfect candidate to replace the Ottoman Empire as the stability-bringing power in the Middle East.

But make no mistake: this book is no apologia for the Saudis either. Nor is it an apologia for Israel. Nor is it an apologia for anyone else in the Middle East, where the old motto very much holds true: the enemy of my enemy is my friend. As a realist, I understand that every country of the Middle East has its own interests and will pursue them. And they are not always interests that you or I will like. But that only underlines why we need to approach the region with clear eyes to see whose interests are most likely to coincide with our own. It is a region I have covered as a reporter for three decades. And as a reporter, I have always concentrated on getting at the truth rather than any politically correct or anodyne fiction.

If you want the hard truth about the Middle East, if you want illusions—which have captivated more than one White House—shattered, if you'd like to know the truth about these oil- and terrorist-rich lands, then read on. We'll take lots of highways and byways—for the region is a mosaic—but in the end, the Middle East will reveal itself as the Hobbesian world that it really is, a world of solitary, poor, nasty, and brutish malcontents, enriched beyond the means of avarice by oil and able to plunge the world into catastrophe, unless a firm hand keeps them in place, as the Ottoman Empire once did.

Chapter 1

BRING BACK THE OTTOMAN EMPIRE

The Middle East a century ago

Think of the Middle East at the start of the twenty-first century: home to the richest, highest quality, most easily accessible oil deposits on earth; cockpit of an extreme Islamist movement that wants to topple moderate regimes and wage aggressive war against the United States and the West; nexus of an unending conflict between Israelis and Palestinians; and widely regarded as the most dangerous area for confrontation between the major powers.

The Middle East is filled with unstable states, none of them more than ninety years old, most of them still suffering from crises of legitimacy. Arab nationalism is a volatile force. The region's birth rate is extraordinarily high, and its rate of population increase vastly exceeds those of the nations of the European Union and Russia. The wealthiest and most strategically desirable real estate in the world is the oil-rich land of southern Iraq, Kuwait, the Gulf States, and the Dhahran region of Saudi Arabia.

But go back a hundred years, and you'll find every one of those conditions reversed. The most backward, remote, and ignored parts of the region were the desert and the coasts of the Arabian (or Persian) Gulf. Neither the Ottoman sultans—who also embodied the caliphate that led

Guess what?

* For hundreds of years the Middle East was the most peaceful part of the world.

* A hundred years ago, the whole world thought the Middle East was useless real estate, especially the Persian Gulf and the Arabian Desert.

* Winston Churchill created Iran's oil industry.

all Islam in Constantinople—nor the chancelleries of any of the great European imperial powers bothered with those wastelands.

In 1905, the region is unified politically and religiously, but the general attitude toward these conditions is one of apathy, lethargy, and resignation. No major oil deposits have been found west of Persia. The caliphate that rules the region and gives it religious direction from Constantinople is ignored or widely despised by most Muslims. The main revolutionary force is a desire among middle-class professionals, students, and intellectuals to establish Western-style parliamentary democracy in the Ottoman Turkish Empire.

At this time, the region is a political, strategic, and economic backwater. None of the great imperial powers of the world regard it as worth a thimble of blood being spilled, let alone oceans of the stuff. There are two tiny Jewish communities in the land still known as Palestine. One contains traditional, extremely observant Jews who, politically, are entirely quiescent. The second, even smaller, consists of weirdly idealistic dreamers—Jewish intellectuals from the czarist Russian Empire who dream of turning themselves into farmers, but are making a bad job of it. Apart from the usual banditry, the land is peaceful and has been for hundreds of years. No one, including the tiny community of Jewish settlers, dreams that this will change for generations. (At the time, David Ben-Gurion, who would become Israel's great founding father, aspired to become a member of an Ottoman Turkish parliament in Istanbul.)

The Ottoman Turkish Empire—the region we call the Middle East today—is lightly populated. Poverty is terrible and universal. Health care, even by the poor American and European standards of the day, is abominable. Even smallpox is still quite common. Public sanitary standards are nonexistent. Infant and child mortality rates are sky-high. Islam as a religion is exceptionally quiescent, passive, and subservient to the political authority of its Ottoman Turkish overlords. The fact that the Ottoman rulers in Constantinople are sultans, and therefore rule their vast empire—more than half the size of the Roman Empire at its greatest extent—as absolute political emperors, is far more important to their subjects than the fact that they also embody the highest religious authority in Islam.

In Palestine, the city of Jerusalem is a backwater, notable for its exceptional beauty from afar and its exceptional filth and poverty, even by regional standards, up close. A handful of Jewish pilgrims come every year to weep in the narrow, fetid alley in front of the last surviving enclosure wall of their ancient temple compound. Jerusalem has been under the firm, unyielding Turkish yoke for almost four hundred years. Nothing has changed. Nothing, it seems, will ever change.

Fast forward a hundred years to the present. Everything has changed. Everything has become the opposite of what it was a century before. How did this happen, and what lessons should we should learn from it?

Ottomans exit, instability and strife enter

For the past ninety years, the defining characteristic of the Middle East has been political instability. European colonial empires, which brought stability to other parts of the world, had little steadying effect here. The heyday of British and the French dominion over the region lasted only twenty-five years—and that included World War II. By 1958, their political and economic influence had been eliminated from Iran, Iraq, Syria, Jordan, Israel, Lebanon, and Egypt. By 1962 the French were gone from Algeria as well, where they had been for more than 130 years. And the Italians had been in Libya so briefly that if you blinked you would have missed them. However brief, European rule over the Middle East was not quiet.

In the interwar years, Syria was rocked by fierce pan-Arab nationalist uprisings against the French, and the British had to put down a full-scale rebellion in Iraq and widespread rioting in Egypt. Under British rule, Iraq and Egypt (the two most populous nations in the region) were never stable, never secure, and never at peace. Throughout the 1920s and 1930s ferocious political intrigues swirled among the British overlords, the local rulers, and the parliamentary democracies installed by the British. In short, Western attempts to impose order on the Middle East failed. What worked in the Americas, Africa, or the rest of Asia did not work here.

In the 1950s, the great tides of anti-Western, anti-imperialist passions swept all these corrupt, incompetent, quasi-parliamentary systems away. They were replaced by regimes modeled on the new great hope of Arab intellectuals—the Socialist Paradise of the Soviet Union. Socialist dictatorships dedicated—at least in theory—to improving the standard of living of the peasant masses were installed in Egypt, Algeria, Libya, Yemen, Syria, and Iraq. Egypt, however, exported instability to much of the rest of the region. Through the 1950s and '60s, Syria and Iraq could not even find a competent dictatorial socialist system to stabilize themselves. By the 1970s, they finally did, but the cost was a level of torture and oppression that exceeded anything the Ottomans had ever resorted to except when they were really mad. In the first decade of the twenty-first century, even this dubious breathing space of stability was starting to break down.

A Book You're Not Supposed to Read

The Emergence of the Middle East, 1914–1924 by Howard M. Sachar; New York: Alfred A. Knopf, 1969. An excellent and far too little read military and political history of World War I and its aftermath in the Middle East, culminating in the abolition of the caliphate.

By contrast, the Ottoman Empire had ruled the whole vast region for four hundred years. There was no Renaissance, no Reformation, no Industrial Revolution, no steady process of improvement and discovery in medicine, hygiene, or public health. After a hundred years as the most powerful empire-state in the world through the sixteenth century, the empire entered a more than three-hundred-year process of long, slow economic and military decline relative to the brawling, dynamic nations of Europe to the northwest. In all that time, the Ottomans' control over the region they had conquered at lightning speed in the first two decades of the sixteenth century was never seriously challenged from within, and it never faltered. When it came to controlling the region and preserving stability, the Ottoman Turks proved far superior to the British and the French in the first half of the twentieth century and to the Americans and Soviets who succeeded them. What was their secret?

The secrets of Ottoman success

When Portuguese explorer Vasco da Gama found a new trade route to the east around the southern end of Africa, and Christopher Columbus and his successors found first the New World and then the way across the Pacific Ocean back to the old one, the Middle East became a global backwater overnight. This provided opportunity for the Ottomans, and they managed it masterfully. There were three key factors.

First, they were locals. Second, they were utterly, relentlessly, and consistently ruthless. Third, they wanted only a quiet life.

Being locals who had already conquered and plundered across the Middle East for half a millennium before they finally came to stay in the early sixteenth century, the Ottoman Turks knew the neighborhood a lot better than the twentieth-century superpowers ever did. They did not think capitalism and democracy would solve all the Middle East's problems, as American idealists from Woodrow Wilson to George W. Bush have. And they did not dream that communism or state socialism (such as the Soviets peddled) would do it either.

Even the Turks' complete indifference to the material well-being of their subjects played to their strengths and was a cause of their success.

They did not obsess about building sewers, dams, or schools as the British and French did. As a result, population remained low, and there was never a baby boom of angry, over-educated teenagers or students rampaging through the streets, shouting, "Turk, go home!"

And even if there had been enough restless, energetic young people to give urban mobs that critical mass, the well-deserved Ottoman Turkish reputation for consistent, merciless slaughter when seriously crossed would have ensured that the mobs stayed at home or, if they were really determined to rape and plunder, found the opportunity to do so by joining the sultan's armies instead.

However, for all their capacity for merciless slaughter, the Ottoman Turks were never, after they won their empire, relentless conquerors or genocidal murderers like Adolf Hitler and Josef Stalin. Unlike Hitler and Stalin—or Saddam Hussein, the one modern Arab ruler nearest to being such a totalitarian monster—the sultan-caliphs did not have an endless, relentless appetite for blood. (The one who came closest, Abdul Hamid II, who massacred Armenians and Bulgarians remorselessly, was also one of the last and most influenced by Western love of "efficiency.")

This was the third secret of their success: they left well enough alone.

And unlike the British in particular, they did not make the mistake of arousing among their subjects vast and undefined dreams of freedom and wealth that they could never have been able to fulfill. In four hundred years, the Ottoman Turkish sultan-caliphs never came up with anything like Magna Carta, the Atlantic Charter, or the Constitution of the United States. That was why they lasted so long.

It also helped that television hadn't been invented yet. But if it had, you can bet the old sultan-caliphs would have kept a tight grip on it. No CNN or al-Jazeera for them.

Finally, for all their status as alien conquerors, the sultans were Muslim, and they embodied the caliphate—that is, they were understood to be the successors to Muhammad's political authority. So they were not religious aliens to most of their subjects. And they also understood—as the British after them certainly did not—that political overlords throughout Islamic history were expected to keep the religious authorities strictly in line. Freedom of religious expression was inconceivable to the sultan-caliphs and to their subjects too. So when the British declined to micromanage local religious preachers on the naïve grounds that as Christians they should leave Islam alone, this was invariably interpreted by every Middle East population under British control as a sign of weakness rather than friendship and tolerance. That helped explain, too, why the British lasted less than a single generation in the neighborhood.

The Ottoman sultans had the formula down. But all empires crumble, and this one was brought down by trendy Westernization and modern ideologies.

The curse of modernity

Ignorance, apathy, and squalor may have been the pillars of the Ottoman Empire, but the result was long-lasting stability and tranquility. The empire's downfall was brought about not by the insidious doings of the big, bad Western empires, but by the trendy shortsightedness of the Turks themselves—specifically, of the handful among them who had read Western books of political thought and made the appalling mistake of taking them seriously.

In 1908, the first and greatest coup of half a century of Middle East coups stripped Sultan Abdul Hamid II in Constantinople of the absolute power he had enjoyed for more than thirty years. Abdul Hamid was notorious in the West for approving horrific massacres of the Christian Armenian community in the empire in 1896. When a group of apparently idealistic, obviously secular, and Western young army officers stripped him of his power to vast national rejoicing, liberal intellectuals and pundits across Europe and America rejoiced too. They were wrong, as usual.

The Young Turks, as the officers called themselves, were the prototype for innumerable similar West-adoring liberal cliques that would spread untold suffering and horror across the Middle East (as well as Asia, Africa, and Latin America) over the next century. For in their passionate enthusiasm to emulate the power of the West as quickly as possible, ancient empires and newly independent former colonial nations alike poured their resources into the training and arming of new armies led by presentable, Westernized young officers. They never stopped to realize that the more they abandoned the ancient customs and stripped such habits and restraints from their new armed forces, the greater would be the likelihood that the arrogant and ambitious young officers might turn their glittering bayonets and—later—shiny new tanks on their own ramshackle political overlords.

The Turks did it before anyone else. The leader of the group was a young officer named Ismail Enver (known as Enver Pasha, "Pasha" being a rank of honor). Enver is nearly unknown in Western circles today except for serious students of history.

Within three years of seizing power, Enver had fought three wars in the Balkans in which tiny, parvenu Balkan nations stripped the empire of ancient provinces it had held for more than five hundred years.

A Book You're Not Supposed to Read

Innocents Abroad by Mark Twain; Mineola, NY: Dover Value Books, 2003. For a vivid, clear-eyed account of the "idyllic" existence of the peoples of the Middle East before the big, bad Western imperialists got there, there is still nothing better. Anyone who wants to see how wonderful life is without sanitation, hygiene, science, and all the other terrible innovations of all those Dead White Males should start here.

Whereas previous Ottoman rulers facing such setbacks had been able to rely on their traditional ally, the British Empire, the landscape was different in the 1900s. By 1908, Britain had fatefully lined up with France and Russia in the Triple Entente to contain Germany, which, with the great Bismarck long since dead, was no longer shy about sticking its nose to the east. Bismarck had declared that nothing in the Balkans was worth the bones of a single dead Pomeranian grenadier. But the man who sacked him as chancellor, Kaiser Wilhelm II, didn't take that advice. He had visions of himself as a modern-day Napoleon bringing enlightenment and progress to the slumbering East. That was as bad an idea for a German emperor as it would prove to be for later U.S. presidents, be their names Wilson, Carter, Clinton, or Bush.

Under Wilhelm, Germany started inching closer to the Ottoman Empire, but was repelled by the corruption, ancient versions of Islamic ritual, and obvious foundering military incompetence that embodied Abdul Hamid's regime.

By contrast, the German kaiser and his generals loved the no-nonsense, (apparently) virile Young Turks, with their dynamic, go-getting new ideas. It proved a marriage made in the infernal regions.

In the six years after 1908, the Young Turks moved at remarkable speed into Imperial Germany's corner, even though it meant making common cause with their most ancient enemy, the Catholic Christian multinational empire of Austria-Hungary under the rule of Emperor Franz Joseph.

The Young Turks had no time for the fuddy-duddy old religious traditions and customs that had defined the Habsburg Empire, like their own, for so long. But like the Habsburgs, they loathed the tiny, aggressive, fierce little nation-states of the Balkans like poison. And they hoped Germany would take care of their most dangerous enemy in modern times, the vast czarist empire of Russia to their north.

So just as Nasser fifty years later would fatefully throw his lot in with the Soviet Union and embark on a policy of military buildup and eventual war against neighboring Israel, Enver Pasha embraced Imperial Germany.

He imported German military advisors to modernize his own army and embarked on a course of confrontation against an England he wrongly thought to be weak and decadent.

World War I could have skipped the Middle East

Ironically, the Ottoman Empire could easily have stayed out of World War I (under the vastly superior, wise leadership of Ismet Inonu, Turkey later stayed out of World War II). The spark that set off the war and that destroyed Europe didn't have to spread to the Middle East—and if not for Enver's bungling, it wouldn't have. Archduke Franz Ferdinand, the fire-breathing and extremely unpleasant heir to the Habsburg Empire, was shot dead on a visit to Sarajevo, capital of the province of Bosnia and Herzegovina, by an idealistic (aren't they all) fanatic young student-killer called Gavrilo Princip.

The assassination triggered calls for war in the highest military and imperial circles in Vienna, Berlin, and St. Petersburg. Franz Joseph was too old, Czar Nicholas II quite simply too stupid, and Kaiser Wilhelm II too weak to stop them.

But the Young Turks, for all their embrace of German generals as military advisors, had no treaty obligations to any of the feuding nations. England had been their traditional ally for more than 120 years since the days of Prime Minister William Pitt the Younger and had saved the empire's bacon on more than one occasion. And England remained, as even Enver understood, the dominant naval power in the Mediterranean Sea.

Then Winston Churchill entered the picture.

In the eight years from 1914 to 1922, there was something fatefully hapless about the young, brilliant, and dynamic Winston Churchill whenever he had to deal with Turkey under its rulers old and new. In all or most of his other dealings with the Middle East, he proved energetic, decisive, visionary, forceful, and even occasionally right. But whenever it came to dealing with the Turks, he always misunderstood them and made them mad.

As part of their ambitious modernization program, the Turks had ordered two new dreadnought battleships from the country most famed for building such things. In 1914, Churchill was still first lord of the admiralty, the civilian head of Britain's fabled Royal Navy, still by far the largest and most powerful in the world. Britain, thanks to Churchill's energy and public advocacy, had a powerful superiority over the Imperial German High Seas Fleet, and her allies France and Japan were among the world's leading naval powers as well. Britain certainly didn't need to seize the two Ottoman/Young Turk battleships being built in its shipyards. It could quietly have concluded some kind of compensation deal with Constantinople in which the ships were either held in British ports until the end

The Fruits of Revolution

"Exhilarated by assurances of a new era of brotherhood and toleration, Turks, Greeks, Arabs, Jews, and Armenians embraced each other in the streets, in public meetings, in joint thanksgiving services."

Howard M. Sachar, *The Emergence of the Middle East,* on the Young Turk Revolution of 1908 in Constantinople

"Suspected traitors and 'counterrevolutionaries' were arrested and deported by the hundreds: execution of political opponents was not unknown."

Sachar on the same government five years later

of the conflict if the Turks agreed to stay neutral, or, if drawn into any conflict with their immediate neighbors, not to use the ships against either Britain or France.

Instead, Churchill immediately went macho. He ordered the battleships seized for Britain's Royal Navy, in which they proved to have less than stellar careers. Reaction across the Ottoman Empire, and not just among the dominant Turks, was immediate. Protest meetings against

Britain were held across the empire. The Young Turk rulers shared the outrage. German diplomats in Constantinople saw their chance and offered to replace the seized battleships at once. But the fly in the ointment was getting any German warship safely to Constantinople, as the British and French navies controlled the Mediterranean.

In the early spring of 1915, however, Churchill and his brilliant but wildly unstable chief of British naval operations, First Sea Lord John "Jackie" Fisher, a septuagenarian hyper-energetic maniac-genius who believed Britain was the lost tribes of Israel, were obsessed with sweeping the raiders and overseas battle squadrons of the Imperial German Navy from the seas. And insofar as they micromanaged British naval dispositions to bottle up the German battle cruisers *Goeben* and *Breslau* in the Mediterranean, they made a hash of it.

At one fateful moment, Rear Admiral Ernest Troubridge, the British squadron commander off the southern tip of Italy, had the chance to trap the *Goeben* and *Breslau* by stationing a heavy cruiser at either end of the Strait of Messina. Instead, he put both the cruisers at the same end and allowed the German warships to sail out unmolested at the other end. On August 10, 1914, the *Goeben* reached safety in the harbor of the Golden Horn at Constantinople, bringing with her, as Churchill later wrote, untold misery and suffering for the peoples of the East. Guaranteed a strong naval force to replace the battleships Britain had seized, Enver and the Young Turks negotiated their fateful alliance with Germany. On October 30, 1914, the Ottoman Empire joined the world war—and thereby ended the centuries-long slumber of the Middle East.

Gallipoli: Underestimating the Turks

At first it seemed that having the Ottoman Empire on their side would be more of a liability to the Germans and the Austrians than an advantage. The British in particular were eager to knock the empire out of the war with a couple of bold moves, and they were sure it could be done. A hastily gathered force from the Indian Army was sent to Basra and started the long slog up the Tigris River valley and through the desert toward Baghdad. It followed exactly the same route that the U.S. armed forces would use with considerably more success and élan eighty-eight years later in 2003. But that wasn't enough for Churchill, who in the spring of 1915 directed his Mediterranean admirals to try to force the strait of the Dardanelles so that their fleet could sail through and put Constantinople, the greatest city of the Ottoman Empire, at the mercy of its heavy naval guns.

After a couple of halfhearted attempts that achieved nothing except to alert the Turkish defenses, the main attempt to force the Dardanelles took place on March 18, 1915. This was indeed, as Churchill recognized in his book *The World Crisis: 1911–1918*, the first, boldest, and best way to knock the Ottoman Empire quickly out of the war, though it is doubtful this would have saved Russia or brought an early end to the slaughter in Europe, as he and his admirers would later maintain. But as it was, Churchill was undone, as he was so often in those days, by his own execrable choice in the admirals he had chosen for high command.

The attacking Anglo-French battle fleet hit minefields in the early waters of the Dardanelles, and in rapid succession three battleships were sunk. The frustration of having their huge battle fleet superiority only a few score miles from the capital of Constantinople, the glittering dream city of the East, was too much for the British War Cabinet. Lord Kitchener, the brutal, energetic, and witless British war minister, was all for landing an army on the Gallipoli peninsula to sweep it free of those pesky batteries and then either advance overland to take Constantinople or finally open the Dardanelles so the fleet could sail through. Churchill was gung-ho for the idea. Neither of them seemed to have bothered looking at a relief map. The Gallipoli peninsula was even worse territory for a slow infantry advance than was the Western Front.

Neither Churchill nor anyone else gave any thought to the problems of landing a huge amphibious force against an enemy armed with modern weapons. The British, Australian, and New Zealand army that came ashore on the beaches of Gallipoli on April 25, 1915, was rowed largely by hand in wooden boats whose sides couldn't stop a single .303 rifle bullet. The waters off the beaches ran thick with blood. No one had yet dreamed of the kind of armored, steel-sided, powered landing craft, or LCT, that the British and Americans would use for all their successful amphibious landings in the European and Pacific theaters in World War II.

Once ashore, there were many more unpleasant surprises in store. The beaches were far smaller and narrower and the hills and cliffs stretching above them far higher and steeper than most of the beaches and hills on the D-Day beaches of Normandy. Tanks hadn't been invented yet. (Churchill in fact would have a major and far happier role in developing them soon.) The British and Anzacs (Australians and New Zealanders) were commanded by an incompetent twit, General Sir Ian Hamilton (a Churchill favorite), while the Turks, who were fighting for their homeland, were led by one of the greatest leaders and generals in their history, Mustafa Kemal, the man later to be known as Ataturk, the father of the Turks.

Kemal had been in the original Young Turk revolutionary group, but was quickly bypassed by Enver and his friends as not being intellectual enough and lacking sufficient "polish." (Like so many murderous incompetents after them, the Young Turks were snobs.) They thought Kemal too abrasive, too intelligent, and too unwilling to flatter them about their own self-imagined "genius." What Kemal thought of them can be concluded from the dungeons and gallows to which he later consigned them.

Unlike them, Kemal also proved to be the one new-generation general who could actually win a major battle. He went on to win lots of them—and against the most modern Western armies.

Kemal was advised by General Otto Liman von Sanders, a brilliant German general of Jewish origin distantly related to the family who owned the American department store Lehman Brothers. Kemal and von

Enver and Nasser: The Losers Everyone Loved

Enver's career bore eerie parallels to that of Gamal Abdel Nasser in Egypt half a century later. Like Nasser, Enver led a tiny group of military officers who espoused vague, idealistic, liberal-romantic political notions and who were revered as liberator-heroes when they seized power, but who really didn't have any idea what to do next.

Nasser, at least, at first took energetic steps to ease the ancient financial and feudal burdens and endless suffering of the poor *fellahin*, or peasants, of the Nile Delta. Enver didn't even manage to do that. Like Nasser he was addicted to giving long, endless speeches to his adoring public but disdained economics and sound business management, and he didn't have a clue how to run or manage his country—which didn't stop him from purging and hounding into exile those who did.

Like Nasser, through a combination of greed, lust for glory, and what he thought was political shrewdness, Enver stumbled into endless foreign wars. But for all his trappings of modernity and radical chic, he was even more hopeless at training or commanding armies in real wars than he was at economics.

Sanders rushed reinforcements up to Gallipoli and kept the allied forces bottled up on the beaches. The allies, spearheaded by the Australians, made passionate efforts to storm the cliffs. It all culminated in the climactic battles at Suvla Bay from August 6 through August 21, 1915.

In *The World Crisis*, Churchill depicts that battle as the Hinge of Fate. Had the Australians been able to hang on, had the British generals managed to gather another company or two of troops, and had the War Cabinet in London shown just a little more backbone, he argued, the heights at Scimitar Hill would have been held, it would have been a downhill-all-the-way sweep to Constantinople, the straits would have been opened at last, and endless, enormous convoys of British, French, and even American munitions would have flooded to Russia to prevent the collapse of the czarist army and prevent the Russian Revolution and all the hecatombs of death and suffering that flowed from it.

The issue remains an important one into the twenty-first century for U.S. policymakers as well as historians and war history enthusiasts. Before Paul Wolfowitz served as American deputy defense secretary from 2001 to 2005, urging the invasion of Iraq, as dean of the Johns Hopkins School for Advanced International Studies in Washington he liked to take favored graduate students on trips to Istanbul to show them how close the Gallipoli campaign—and Churchill's vision—came to changing the course of twentieth-century history.

But in reality, without tanks, trucks, and the tactical doctrine and training to carry out rapid armored war, the British couldn't have hoped to advance at more than a crawl and the Turks would have fought them all the way and kept them bottled up. Also, the thirty-mile Gallipoli peninsula continues with hilly, ravine territory for miles beyond the landing beaches. Winning the battles at Suvla Bay and Scimitar Hill would just have been the prelude to endless bloodbaths of the kind already occurring on the Western Front. And by the time Suvla Bay was fought in August 1915, the Russian army had already lost millions dead on the Eastern Front and been forced out of Poland. Russia's collapse by then was inevitable.

Lessons of Gallipoli

The British defeat at Gallipoli in 1915, and the much smaller one at Kut that same year, taught lessons to Western nations about getting entangled in the Middle East that are more relevant now than ever.

First, local populations and nations in the region should not be despised or underestimated just because they have lost wars for scores or hundreds of years. Every war is different. The British and the Arab nations chronically underestimated the Jewish community in Palestine in 1947–1948, and Israelis underestimated the Egyptians and the Syrians in 1973.

Second, battles, wars, and military campaigns can be very easy to start but very hard to stop. Once you're in, you're in, and a campaign takes on a mad life of its own, sucking in unimagined resources as casualties soar and the deadlock deepens. The United States has been learning that in Iraq.

Third, local populations that perform miserably in the face of one kind of war can prove formidably brilliant in another kind of conflict. The Turks failed miserably when they attempted offensive operations against the British in Sinai in 1915 and 1916 and against the Russians around Lake Van. But when they had to fight a straightforward defensive struggle to protect their ancestral heartland at Gallipoli, or later against the invading Greek army in 1920–1921, Turkish peasant soldiers proved to be the epitome of courage, resilience, and toughness—and they won.

That lesson applies to twenty-first-century Iraq too. The Iraqi army, even at the height of its power in 1991, proved useless against the attack of a vast U.S. and allied force commanded by General Norman Schwarzkopf. It proved equally helpless against the lightning thrusts of the U.S.

Army and Marines in the 2003 campaign. Yet the same soldiers had fought superbly and successfully against Iranian human wave attacks in the 1980–1988 Iran-Iraq War just a few years before. And when it came to a guerrilla war against U.S. forces with infinitely superior firepower from May 2003 on, the Sunni Muslim insurgents in Iraq proved to be innovative, adaptive, ruthless, and utterly relentless.

Europe's "sick man" has some teeth

For more than a century before the start of World War I, the great Christian empires of Europe looked upon the Ottoman Empire as the "Sick Man of Europe"—a rotting edifice that would collapse if any serious power went to war against it. This widespread assumption lay behind the naïvely romantic belief among young British officers who sailed off to the Gallipoli campaign in 1915 that it would combine the epic heroism of the Trojan War with the gallantry and triumphs of the early Crusades.

But the British quickly learned the hard way that if the Ottoman Turkish Empire was a sick old man, it was a sick old man with teeth that still delivered a nasty bite.

Winston Churchill's visionary campaign to knock Turkey out of the war with a single blow was drowned in blood. The Turkish conscript soldiers led by Kemal fought with ferocious bravery and kept the British, Australian, and New Zealand divisions pinned down on their tiny beachhead. Later the same year, an Anglo-Indian army of 10,000 men led by Sir Charles Townshend marched up from the Persian Gulf to take Baghdad but was blocked by strong, unanticipated Ottoman resistance. Townshend, rather than sensibly retreat back to the safety of Kuwait on the coast, sat still for long, fatal weeks in the town of Kut while the Turks slowly but steadily built up their forces and cut off his line of retreat.

The double British humiliations of Gallipoli and Kut smashed the old myth of the weak, corrupt, and cowardly old Turks. They put the British on the defensive, licking their wounds. It would be two years before far larger, better organized British armies started the laborious task of rolling up the Ottoman Empire in the Middle East from its extremities, driving into Palestine from Egypt and back into Mesopotamia, modern Iraq, from Kuwait.

But the British disasters at Gallipoli and Kut taught an important lesson that British policymakers quickly forgot—and that twenty-first-century U.S. policymakers forgot too. However backward they might superficially appear by Western standards, the societies of the Middle East have a strength, identity, and resilience of their own. Conquering them and reshaping them is often a far tougher job than it appears at first sight.

Chapter 2

THE ARAB-ISRAELI CONFLICT
It's Not Israel's Fault

The Arab-Israeli conflict today isn't about borders and never was. It's about a struggle for existence. The origins of the conflict indeed lie in the post–World War I happenings in the region, but beyond that, the commonly understood history of this conflict is riddled with politically correct myths and misconceptions.

Academia and the media like to say the strife began with the extraordinary 1967 Six-Day War, and Israel's conquest of the Gaza Strip, the West Bank, eastern Jerusalem, and the Golan Heights. That war (which was a preemptive but defensive war by Israel), was part of a larger war that had started half a century earlier.

The creation of Israel: An anti-Muslim U.S. conspiracy?

If you believe the rhetoric of the average Muslim agitator today, Israel is the unholy spawn of the Great Satan—the United States. In fact, the first president to address the issue was Woodrow Wilson, who was hostile to the idea of a "Jewish national home in Palestine."

The idea of Israel had its real advocates among the British, who in 1917 issued the famous Balfour Declaration, calling for the creation of a Jewish state. This was not out of British love for the Jews and the Zionists among

Guess what?

- An intrigue of British anti-Semites made a future Nazi ally the religious leader of the Palestinian Arabs—and the Palestinians didn't want him.

- When it came to maintaining law and order, the British ran Palestine worse than the Ottoman Turks ever did.

- The Arab states openly declared their determination to prevent a Jewish state from being born in 1947—twenty years before the West Bank and Gaza were first occupied.

them. (*Zionist* is a loaded word, to be sure, but it literally means someone who believes in a Jewish state.) The Balfour Declaration was actually based on the ludicrous belief that the Zionist leaders of the time controlled the Bolshevik Revolution in Russia and the political destiny of the United States. The Zionists, who knew their own powerlessness, never dreamed they held such influence or aspired to anything of the sort.

In autumn 1917 the British War Cabinet faced a dire prospect. Russia was floundering and on the verge of being knocked out of the war, and it would be many months, perhaps more than a year, before new American armies could be trained, transported, and organized to plug the holes on the weakened Western Front. How could Britain keep Russia on its feet and America committed in the meantime?

Sir Mark Sykes, Britain's chief diplomatic negotiator on Middle East affairs, had an answer. In flowering, ecstatic language that reads more like a bad Victorian novel than sober documents of state, he proclaimed that the Zionist movement had vast power over the Bolsheviks in Russia and over the government of President Woodrow Wilson in the United States. Commit the British cause to establishing a Jewish homeland in Palestine, and "Great Jewry" would make sure Russia stayed in the war while speeding up America's commitment to send its armies to the Western Front. The desperate government of Prime Minister David Lloyd George, ready to clutch at straws, bought into this fevered fantasy.

None of this kooky calculation was known to Chaim Weizmann, the head of the Zionist movement in Britain. He genuinely thought that the growing British interest in his cause was based on a passion for the Bible and justice for the Jews, as well as on gratitude for his own useful role in building modern munitions factories the length of Britain to provide more shells for the war.

If Weizmann had known what was truly motivating the British embrace of Zionism, he would have laughed. It was true that there were a disproportionate number of Jews among the Bolshevik leadership, most

An Unlikely Friendship

In 1919, David Ben-Gurion, like many other romantic liberal nationalists from the most obscure parts of Europe, Asia, and the Middle East, came to Paris hoping to advocate his people's case for nationhood to U.S. president Woodrow Wilson (no friend of the Zionists, to put it mildly) and to the Versailles Peace Conference. Paris was packed solid with similar hopefuls and apartment space was at a premium, so Ben-Gurion stayed in the same hotel as another impecunious young romantic idealist. They became fast friends. And the young Ho Chi Minh, future leader of a ferocious rebellion against France and then Communist ruler of North Vietnam, assured Ben-Gurion that if the British dashed his hopes, there would always be room for the Jewish national home in his independent, democratic Republic of Vietnam.

notably Leon Trotsky. But they were a tiny minority among their own people and—as good Communists—they hated every form of Jewish nationalism. Throughout the seventy-four years of Soviet history, any form of Jewish nationalist or Zionist organization was mercilessly suppressed by successive Soviet regimes.

The idea that Woodrow Wilson was in Weizmann's pocket was even more ludicrous. Wilson, for all his talk of national self-determination, was highly selective and arbitrary about which nationalities he empowered and which he ignored or repressed. He never showed any sympathy for the Jewish national home policy and later sent envoys to Palestine who opposed it ferociously. The first U.S. president to publicly and explicitly state his support for the establishment of a Jewish national home in Palestine was Wilson's successor, Warren G. Harding.

Mark Sykes died of the Spanish flu in 1919, having made his mark on history. Successive generations of Jewish Zionists and Israelis revered him as a great friend and benefactor. Almost none of them knew that it was his cavalier acceptance of some of the worst anti-Semitic myths that put him at their side.

How it all began

The roots of the Arab-Israeli conflict lie in the 1917–1920 period. Such conflict was unavoidable. The Jewish people had a hereditary presence in Palestine going back more than three thousand years. There had always been significant numbers of Jews there, especially in Jerusalem. But after the British government committed itself to the Jewish national home policy, Palestinian Arab opposition to the returning Jewish community was unrelenting.

This might not have mattered if the British ran their empire the way the Romans or the Ottomans had: boldly declaring their policies and pushing them through, regardless of resistance. But the British conquerors did not behave as conquerors. Anti-Semitic prejudice was rampant in the British Army's Occupied Enemy Territories Administration, which ruled Palestine from 1917 to 1920. During those fateful years, officers and administrators at the highest level of the British bureaucracy gave encouragement, protection, and promotion to the most murderous and extreme anti-Jewish Palestinian leaders. Not surprisingly, their favorites turned out to be equally vicious enemies of the British as well.

One favorite anti-Israel claim is that the creation of Israel meant driving Arabs from the Holy Land. In truth, there was room for both populations to live side by side. Historian David Fromkin estimates the Palestinian Arab population in 1917–1918 at 600,000, which may be far too high. The territory of Palestine had been ravaged by more than four years of war and by a fierce famine that killed thousands of Arabs and Jews alike. (The great Jewish scholar Gershom Scholem recalled in his memoirs more than half a century later that when he first came to

Jerusalem he was able to buy huge numbers of rare, ancient books on Jewish mysticism in Jerusalem because the holy men and their families who had owned them had died of hunger and disease during the war. Palestinian Arab peasants had died in even greater numbers.)

Palestine had not been a totally empty, deserted land under the Turks, but it was certainly a very lightly populated one. In 1881, before any modern significant Jewish immigration from the czarist Russian Empire began, in very small numbers for the next thirty-three years, the total population was certainly less than half a million.

Ironically, illegal Arab immigration into Palestine during the post–World War I period of British rule (known as the Mandate), largely overland from

PC Myth: It's All about the Palestinian Refugees

Of all the myths about the Arab-Israeli conflict, this one is by far the most prevalent. The plight of the Palestinians—Arabs and Jews—was certainly horrendous at the end of the 1947–1948 war. But if there had been no war, there would have been no refugees at the end of it.

An estimated 700,000 Palestinian refugees were created by the war, according to UN estimates made right after it. This was almost exactly the same figure as the number of Sephardic Jews who were expelled from their ancient homes throughout the Arab world in the backlash wave of persecutions that followed the establishment of Israel. Almost all of them ended up going to the Jewish state.

It should also be noted that in the nightmarish years from 1945 to 1948, at least thirty million refugees were created by the end of World War II in Europe, the redrawing of national boundaries that followed, and the horrific massacres and war between Hindus and Muslims in the 1947 partition of India. So the real outcome of the 1947–1948 war was a massive, though far from unprecedented, transfer of population between Israel and the Arab world.

Syria and Iraq, may have exceeded the number of Jews immigrating into the country in absolute numbers at the same time. The British limited the number of Jewish immigrants based on presumed economic absorptive capacity if the land. This basically meant the government's Jewish Agency and the Jewish organizations running and encouraging the settlement had to provide the economic infrastructure for immigrants before they arrived.

But the growing prosperity of the urban economy also attracted large numbers of Arab peasants from neighboring countries. The British never bothered cracking down on them; they didn't have enough troops to close the land borders even if they wanted to. As a result, Jewish investment also ended up significantly strengthening the Palestinian Arab urban population.

The rise of Haj Amin al-Husseini

For the entire troubled length of the British military occupation and Mandate in Palestine from 1917 to 1947, the figure of Haj Amin al-Husseini, the mufti (Muslim religious leader) of Jerusalem, blocked the paths of the British and Zionist Jewish settlers. If you're seeking a source of the strife and hatred in the Arab-Israeli conflict, this British-picked mufti is a good place to look.

Husseini, a cousin of Yasser Arafat, was even more murderous toward his own people than he was toward the British and the Palestinian Jews. Once he was in office, it never occurred to the British occupiers—as it would certainly have occurred to their Ottoman Turkish predecessors—to simply remove him from office or kill him.

This misplaced constitutionality queasiness was quickly grasped by Husseini and his followers, encouraging the mufti to defy with impunity the British rulers who had appointed him in the first place.

Husseini was no serious Islamic cleric. He was simply a handsome young junior notable from one of the two or three most prominent Palestinian families in the highlands of Palestine. He was able to rise to the top despite his youth and inexperience because he curried favor with the British, especially with Sir Ernest Richmond, the chief architect of the British administration in Jerusalem, who also happened to be fiercely anti-Semitic and ultra-reactionary.

Richmond prevailed upon his long-term lover, Sir Ronald Storrs (the same intriguing official who had drafted the infamous correspondence with Sherif Hussein in Mecca in 1915–1916 and then garbled their plain meaning because of his linguistic incompetence). Storrs had been promoted to governor of Jerusalem, where he got Richmond an influential job as assistant secretary to the

Books You're Not Supposed to Read

O Jerusalem by Larry Collins and Dominique Lapierre; New York: Simon and Schuster, 2007.

Genesis 1948: The First Arab-Israeli War by Dan Kurzman; New York: Da Capo Press, 1992.

Two highly readable, superbly researched, and even-handed books first published nearly forty years ago and still unrivaled introductions to the ferocious nature of the 1947–1948 war.

British ruler of Palestine, High Commissioner Sir Herbert Samuel. Samuel was Jewish, but more importantly, he was a high-minded, do-gooding liberal fool who later opposed Churchill's warnings about the rise of Nazi Germany. Samuel naïvely followed Richmond's recommendation and passed over better qualified candidates to appoint the dignified, handsome, impeccably mannered—but also psychopathically genocidal and murderous—young Husseini to the job. Tens of thousands of innocent Arabs and Jews were to die so that Samuel could feel high-minded and morally superior.

Thereafter, for more than a quarter of a century, successive British administrators deferred to Husseini as if he were the archbishop of Canterbury.

He was nothing of the kind. First, he orchestrated a campaign of assassination and terror to cow the Nashashibi clan, the moderate extended family of notables who were the Husseinis' ancient rivals. Then, pioneering a form of diplomacy his cousin Arafat would adopt on a grand scale, he internationalized and Islamicized the native Palestinian Arab opposition to the Jewish settlement in Palestine. He took advantage of the 1929 riots in Jerusalem to claim that the Jews were plotting to destroy the Dome of the Rock and the al-Aqsa Mosque. The governments of surrounding Arab nations Egypt, Iraq, and Saudi Arabia, eager to distract their own populations from domestic issues and establish their own credentials, followed Husseini's lead. By 1936, when the main Palestinian Arab revolt began against the British rulers and the Jewish Zionist settlers, Husseini was the undoubted dominant figure among Palestinian Arabs.

He was a disaster for his people, but he was also popular among them. Like any native population faced with the sudden appearance of European colonists, Palestinians rose up in defiance, fiercely opposing the Jewish settlement and the British policy of supporting it. A century of war might well have been inevitable in any case. But the fact remains that Husseini was far more extreme, murderous, and unrelenting than the

How the Conspiracy Theorists Created Israel

"To my mind, the Zionists are now the key of the situation—the problem is, how are they to be satisfied? With 'Great Jewry' against us there is no possible chance of getting the thing thro'—it means optimism in Berlin, dumps in London, unease in Paris, resistance to last ditch in C'nople [Constantinople], dissension in Cairo, Arabs all squabbling among themselves. As Shakespeare says, 'Untune that string and mark what discord follows.'"

Sir Mark Sykes, chief British diplomatic negotiator on the Middle East, to Sir Arthur Nicolson, permanent under-secretary for foreign affairs, March 18, 1916

Nashashibis, who were the most likely alternative. He also flatly refused to enter even the most cautious and exploratory of negotiations with any Jewish leaders at every step.

By 1929, using the issues of the Dome of the Rock and al-Aqsa in Jerusalem, Husseini had stirred up opposition to Jewish settlement throughout the Muslim world. Violent Arab riots broke out in 1929 when scores of Jews were killed around Palestine.

Finally, in 1936, a popular Arab revolt broke out against the Jewish settlement. Husseini took advantage of this revolt, which he had worked hard to foment, to use terror gangs he controlled to assassinate all his potential rivals. For the next eleven years he was the unrivalled leader of the Palestinian Arab community and the worst they ever had. Finally, in 1939, the British sent a then unknown general, Bernard Montgomery, who defeated the revolt.

A Book You're Not Supposed to Read

Inside the Anglo-Arab Labyrinth by Elie Kedourie; Oxford: Routledge Publishers, 2000.

In World War II, Husseini took the logical ultimate step to becoming an eager accessory—and a very effective one—to the most monstrous crime in history: he spent the war years in Fascist Italy and Nazi Germany. He was very active in urging the SS bureaucrats running the Final Solution, the methodically planned genocide of the entire Jewish people in Europe, to make sure that children, especially from the Sephardic Jewish communities of the Balkans, were not spared from the gas chambers in Auschwitz. He recruited SS regiments for the Nazis from the Bosnian Muslim community in Yugoslavia. They guarded the security of the railway lines carrying cattle trucks filled with hundreds of thousands of Balkan Jews for the extermination chambers and cremation ovens of Auschwitz. One of those forces took a leading role in the genocide of hundreds of thousands of Serbs and Gypsies, as well as Jews, in Yugoslavia.

Husseini was also a close personal friend of Adolf Eichmann and Heinrich Himmler. He even visited Auschwitz on at least one occasion to make sure the job was being done right.

When the great showdown between the Jews and Arabs in Palestine that he had lusted for finally came in 1947, Haj Amin al-Husseini's unrelenting policy of seeking to drive every Jew into the sea led instead to the shattering and scattering of his own people. Posing as their greatest champion, he repeatedly proved himself to be their greatest calamity.

Churchill in Cairo: 1921

He came. He was photographed alongside his friends sitting on a camel. He painted the Pyramids. He summoned his heroes T. E. Lawrence and Gertrude Bell to meet with him. When Winston Churchill visited Cairo in 1921 as His Majesty's secretary of state for the colonies, he had the kind of holiday little boys dream of. He also drew the map of the modern Middle East.

Three modern Middle East nations were created by the decisions Churchill made and the lines he drew at the epochal Cairo Conference.

First, he upheld the already highly controversial policy to establish a Jewish national home in Palestine and to build it up with massive immigration from the impoverished and persecuted Jewish communities of Europe. That policy ultimately ensured the creation of the State of Israel.

Second, Churchill unilaterally recognized as-Sayyid Abdullah as the real presence on the ground east of the Jordan River. Abdullah, the eldest son of that old British favorite Sherif Hussein of Mecca, was the emir (prince) of Transjordan

Of all the Hashemites at that time, Abdullah was the one British rulers and policymakers liked least—perhaps because he was the smartest and wasn't prepared to dance at their every word. But the British didn't need the embarrassment of kicking him out of Transjordan, and they needed to set up some kind of government to keep the peace on the cheap. So Abdullah stayed.

Third, Churchill created the modern nation-state of Iraq under King Faisal I. It had never existed in history unless you count the famous but brief Babylonian Empire of Nebuchadnezzar 2,400 years earlier. But the British were determined to hold on to the fabulously oil-rich territories they had finally conquered with such difficulty in the closing period of World War I. And the great 1920 Shiite revolt in southern Iraq had underlined the urgent need to establish some kind of native Arab government supposedly acceptable to the people of Mesopotamia. A friendly native government was needed because the British lacked the financial resources or the will to occupy the land militarily. Being able to produce Faisal, another son of Sherif Hussein, as the "king of the Arabs" was thus a political masterstroke for Churchill.

In the short term, the huge redrawing of the Middle East map that Churchill decreed at Cairo proved, especially from the British point of view, an outstanding success. For the next eighty years, ultra-right Jewish and Zionist nationalists attacked the "treachery" of cutting off Jordan—more than half the territory Britain controlled after World War I. But almost no Jews lived in the Transjordan territories when Churchill gave them to Abdullah, and the British lacked the military manpower to enforce Jewish settlement

A Question of Numbers

Was Palestine empty when the Balfour Declaration was announced and the Jewish national home policy declared? No, it certainly was not.

Was there room for millions of Jewish immigrants to settle there without displacing the Arab inhabitants. Yes, there certainly was.

"The Zionists pictured Palestine— correctly as we now know—as a country that could support at least five to ten times more people than lived there at the time; so that without displacing any of the perhaps 600,000 Arab inhabitants there was room to bring in millions of Jewish settlers."

David Fromkin, *A Peace to End All Peace*

Well, If It's Good for the British Empire...

"It is manifestly right that the scattered Jews should have a national center and a national home to be reunited. And where else but Palestine, with which for three thousand years they have been intimately and profoundly associated? We think it will be good for the world, good for the Jews, good for the British Empire, but also good for the Arabs who dwell in Palestine...(for) we intend that they shall share in the benefits and progress of Zionism."

Winston Churchill, British colonial secretary, speaking to a delegation of Muslim Arabs in Jerusalem on March 30, 1921

there anyway. There weren't even enough Jewish settlers coming from Central and Eastern Europe to develop Palestine at the time. In the early 1920s the British Colonial Office was furious at the Zionist Organization for bringing in too few Jewish settlers.

In the event, Palestine enjoyed one of its brief interludes of peace for eight years after the Cairo Conference, and the British Parliament somewhat reluctantly accepted the Lloyd George-Churchill-Balfour policy of encouraging Jewish immigration and building up the Jewish national home.

Even in Iraq, the news seemed to get better; the Shiite revolt was finally crushed and the British slowly prepared Iraq for a form of titular independence under Faisal while keeping the reins of power firmly in their own hands.

But twenty years after Churchill's hour of triumph in Cairo, the Arab houses of cards he had so flamboyantly created came crashing down on his head. In the spring of 1941, with General Erwin Rommel's Afrika Korps charging across the Western Desert toward Egypt, Britain stood alone and isolated against the Nazi conquerors of Europe. At this moment, the officers of the Iraqi army that had been painstakingly crafted for twenty years to do Britain's will in the Middle East rose in revolt, kicked the British out, and declared that Iraq was joining the Axis. Pro-Nazi forces also took over in French-controlled Syria next door. At this darkest hour for Britain's imperial fortunes in the Middle East, even most of the famous

Arab Legion of Transjordan, led by a British officer, John Glubb, passively mutinied and refused to march against their pro-Nazi Arab brothers in Iraq.

Churchill in 1921 as colonial secretary had created Iraq and Jordan to secure the British Empire in the Middle East. Twenty years later, as Britain's embattled war premier, he found the armies of both nations stabbing Britain in the back when it needed them most. Only the Jews of Palestine, who had no reason by then to love the British, but who had nowhere else to go, provided the last stronghold from which the British could decisively strike back and briefly regain their mastery of the Middle East.

But in the twenty-first century, the lines that Churchill drew so confidently on a map in Cairo in 1921 continue to shape the history of the world. The militarily powerful little state of Israel that grew out of his Jewish national home policy continues to struggle for survival against enemies close at hand and, in the case of Iran, at the far end of the region. And the artificiality of the unity he imposed on Iraq now bedevils U.S. policymakers even more than it did British ones. Churchill's Cairo legacy therefore remains a mixed one, to put it mildly.

Emir Abdullah of Transjordan

The British experience with Middle Eastern nation-building and ruler-picking could have taught the West this much: a good man is hard to find—and sometimes hard to recognize when you've got him.

During their brief imperial heyday in the Middle East, the British displayed an uncanny talent for choosing and empowering the biggest losers (like King Faisal of Iraq and Sherif Hussein of Mecca) and the most poisonous, unrelenting enemies (like Haj Amin al-Husseini, the mufti of Jerusalem) while despising or opposing successful rulers of real ability like Mustafa Kemal Ataturk in Turkey or King Abdulaziz ibn Saud in

The Mufti and the Nazis

"The mufti was one of the initiators of the systematic extermination of European Jewry and had been a collaborator and advisor of Eichmann and Himmler in the execution of his plan....He was one of Eichmann's best friends and had constantly incited him to accelerate the extermination measures. I heard him say that accompanied by Eichmann, he had visited incognito the gas chambers of Auschwitz."

Dieter Wisliceny, senior SS officer and a key executioner of the Final Solution

Saudi Arabia. The only time they hit on a real winner, they did so in spite of themselves.

Even when Winston Churchill gave Emir Abdullah, the eldest son of Sherif Hussein, rule over Transjordan to shut him up and keep the territory quiet in 1921, nothing much was expected from him. In the eyes of Churchill, Abdullah was the least of the Hashemites. They still clung to the ridiculous fantasy that the whole Arab Muslim world regarded, or would come to regard, Sherif Hussein in Mecca as the successor of the Ottoman caliphs in Constantinople. And their hearts beat faster thinking of Faisal as the dashing new pro-British, enlightened ruler who would usher in a new Golden Age—under British tutelage, naturally—in Baghdad. (Eighty years later, Bush administration policymakers would go weak in the knees over Iraqi National Congress leader Ahmed Chalabi the same way).

Abdullah—small, shrewd, not very handsome, and always soft-spoken—was in their eyes the least of the three. But he would outlast them all.

There was no oil in Jordan. And for more than half a century after the emirate was created, even the tourist traffic to see its wonderful antiquities was negligible. But Abdullah was sober, intelligent, industrious, and street-smart. He worked quietly with the British to keep order and with only a fraction of the state budget of neighboring Iraq handled it with conspicuously greater success. Commerce boomed, and the lazy village of Amman, where Abdullah and his Bedouin had encamped in 1920, grew to become a major regional city.

As this book goes to press, Abdullah's great-grandson, King Abdullah II, continues to rule over a kingdom of Jordan that against all odds has survived hostile neighbors on every side to become and remain—without benefit of any oil revenues—a relatively prosperous nation and one of the safest and most stable in the entire Middle East over the past century.

Emir Abdullah's heirs outlasted the British, the French, and the Soviet Union. They also outlasted old Sherif Hussein, humiliatingly kicked out of Mecca only a few years after the Cairo Conference by Abdulaziz ibn Saud, the real warrior hero and statesman whom Churchill, Bell, and T. E. Lawrence "of Arabia" had no time for. Abudullah's heirs have already by almost half a century outlasted the kingdom of Iraq—Churchill's pride and joy—and Faisal's heirs, whom the Iraqi army shot in cold blood in the horrific military coup of 1958.

The success and longevity of Abdullah and his heirs—contrasted with the failures of Churchill's handpicked rulers elsewhere in the region—ought to be a lesson to the West: in the Middle East, our ideas of what a leader should be are often wrong.

Herbert Dowbiggin: Unlikely prophet

Herbert Dowbiggin was a career colonial police administrator of the British Empire who ran the police force of Ceylon—today the nation of Sri Lanka—with an iron fist from 1913 to 1937. He had hardly any interest in the Middle East and was sent out to report on why the Palestine police failed to deter the bloody riots of 1929 that resulted in the massacre of hundreds of Jews, especially in the town of Hebron. But amid all the visionary lunatics and ambitious, bungling, two-faced administrators and politicians who got everything wrong for half a century and then obsessively tried to cover up their tracks, Dowbiggin stands out as a breath of common sense and sound advice.

Dowbiggin's 1930 report was one of the most important and valuable studies on maintaining law and order in occupied or colonial nations ever written. He insisted that every minority community at possible risk from an attack, riot, or pogrom by the alienated majority had to have its own armed police detachment. He emphasized the importance of maintaining excellent roads and telephone communications between outlying police stations and the capital, and of having fast-reacting reserves of police who could quickly be sent to trouble spots. Most of all, he emphasized the importance of having a very large, well-trained police force whose highly visible presence on the ground deterred violence from breaking out in the first place.

There is a remarkably modern ring to Dowbiggin's insistence that colonial disorders—in Palestine as well as in Ceylon—needed to be handled as policing operations, not military ones. Israeli military historian Martin van Creveld has said the reasons the British security forces were so effective against the Irish Republican Army in the Northern Ireland conflict was that they dealt with it as a policing operation, not a military one. Using armies as armies automatically causes a lot of collateral damage, including lots of civilian casualties. And the more innocent civilians are killed and injured, the broader the popular support for the guerrilla movement becomes.

But as is so often the case with true prophets, as opposed to the more common false ones, Dowbiggin's warnings fell on deaf ears. Sir Charles Tegart, who took over the Palestine police in the 1930s, ignored Dowbiggin's report and militarized the police, moving them into breathtaking mountaintop barracks that were twentieth-century versions of Crusader castles. They had the same fate. After a little more than a decade in the Tegart Forts, as they were called, the British were forced to evacuate Palestine. By 1947 they had lost all effective political support among Palestinian Arabs and Jews alike.

But to this day, Dowbiggin's report remains the most important document for any Western policymaker grappling with the tactical problems of maintaining law and order in an occupied society.

How British imperialist weakness sparked the Arab-Israeli conflict

The British did a lot for both the Arabs and the Jews during the thirty years they ruled Palestine. The population of the country tripled. Prosperity unknown since Roman times arrived. Swamps were drained and modern sanitation, hospitals, and schools were built for both communities. The only thing lacking was law and order.

On April 4, 1920, less than a year and half after World War I had ended, an anti-Jewish pogrom swept through the streets of the Old City of Jerusalem. A number of Jews were killed and hundreds wounded. In four hundred years of Ottoman Turkish rule, such a thing had not happened once.

Under the hand of a kinder, gentler empire, the Jewish people were more threatened than they ever had been under the tough Muslim empire that preceded it. The British were unable to keep the peace, and such anti-Jewish violence happened again and again, with growing ferocity and exponentially larger casualties on each occasion.

Churchill on Holiday

"He seems to have gone to Cairo in something of a holiday mood. His juniors complained that he would delay briefing himself with important papers while he concentrated on the more congenial task of writing *The World Crisis*, and they criticized him for setting apart so much time for painting Egyptian and Palestinian landscapes."

Christopher Sykes in *Crossroads to Israel*, describing Winston Churchill at the Cairo Conference

The first civilian governor the British set up to rule Palestine after they ended their brief, disastrous period of military occupation there was idealistic liberal party leader Sir Herbert Samuel, who was Jewish.

In classic liberal fashion, Samuel tried to turn his country's enemies into friends by showing them mercy and kindness. What he reaped instead was an entire generation of civil strife and bloodshed as a result. Thousands of innocents on both sides would pay with their lives for Sir Samuel's progressive high-mindedness.

The Hebrew Bible: A book of war

"Wingate: there was a man of genius who could have been a man of destiny."

Winston Churchill paid that tribute to British brigadier general Orde Wingate after he was killed in a plane crash in Burma in 1944. Churchill was right about the genius (it takes one to know one), but he didn't realize that in his short, extraordinary life, Wingate had already decisively reshaped the future of the world—especially the Middle East.

Wingate was a brilliant young British army officer and biblical fundamentalist Christian zealot who was posted to Palestine as a young captain in 1936 at the start of the Arab Revolt. He had shown no especial interest in either Jews or Zionism before going there, but quickly became obsessed with the potential of the young pioneer Jewish community and became convinced it was God's will that a Jewish state be restored in Palestine after thousands of years. He also believed that he was personally destined to raise its army and lead it in battle. These views were understandably received with some surprise, not to mention suspicion, by both British military commanders and Jewish community leaders in the Mandate.

However, as a few thousand Arab guerrillas continued to run rings around what at one point constituted 25 percent of the active combat force of the British army, both groups became increasingly desperate. Wingate got the approval to raise from Jewish volunteers what became known as his Special Night Squads (SNS) to defend the British oil pipeline from Iraq to the Palestine port of Haifa. He imprinted on them his own highly unorthodox and idiosyncratic combat doctrines, primarily inspired not by Carl von Clausewitz and the German or French general staffs, but by a close reading of the Old Testament, the Hebrew Bible.

Sounds Like Pre-Giuliani New York

"Public security, particularly in the north, is almost non-existent....Neither Jews nor Arabs have any confidence in the (British) authorities....The older inhabitants say that public security was far better maintained under the Turks."

The Times, August 10, 1921 (quoted in David Fromkin, *A Peace to End All Peace*)

Wingate drew tactical lessons and doctrines from the campaigns and victories of such biblical heroes as Joshua, Gideon, and David. He emphasized the importance of small, fast-moving commando forces who were tough, motivated, and trained to know intimately the areas in which they operated. He emphasized night marches through difficult and mountainous terrain to take the enemy by surprise. He loved night attacks. According to some testimonies much later, Wingate also advocated extreme ruthlessness in the shooting of suspects or random victims taken from villages from which terrorists had launched their attacks.

His SNS played a crucial role in damaging the morale of the Palestinian Arab guerrilla bands operating in the Galilee region of Israel during the last year of the Arab Revolt—a role far out of proportion to their numbers. But they were too few to crush the revolt. That was carried out by much larger and more widespread British forces and operations commanded by a tough new senior commander, Major General Bernard Law Montgomery. In 1939, British senior commanders, recognizing Wingate's

43

passionate identification with the Jewish community, transferred him out of Palestine. There were standing orders that he never be allowed to serve there again.

But, thankfully for Israel, it was too late. Wingate had already provided invaluable military education to a crucial number of the first, defining generation of senior officers in what would become the Israel Defense Forces. His young soldiers and students included men who would become the greatest generals in Israel's wars of survival in the first twenty years of its existence: Moshe Dayan, Yigael Allon, and Yitzhak Rabin.

PC Myth: The Twice-Promised Land

Did the British cynically promise the Holy Land to both the Arabs and the Jews? That's the popular history—and it's false. In 1916, Sir Mark Sykes had concluded a secret agreement on partitioning the spoils of the Ottoman Empire with his French counterpart, Francois Georges-Picot. Considering that the British army was held within the Battle of the Somme that year and the French army was suffering more horrific casualties defending the fortress of Verdun, this was certainly an exercise in wishful thinking. History books and Mideast commentators like to portray the Sykes-Picot Agreement as the archetypal Western betrayal of Muslims, and they trace Eastern mistrust of Europe to this agreement. But in reality it was neither monstrous nor unprecedented in the conduct of states.

The Sykes-Picot Agreement, in the eyes of liberal and Third World commentators, was a cynical betrayal of solemn promises that the British had made only the year before to Sherif Hussein of Mecca, guardian of the

continued on next page

continued from previous page

Muslim holy places. The British governor general of the Sudan, Sir Henry McMahon, had offered all of Palestine to the Arabs.

McMahon certainly signed the letters, written in Arabic, sent to Hussein. But they were in no way a treaty obligation and, far more to the point, Palestine was not remotely promised in them.

Later generations of British and Arab historians pored over the McMahon-Hussein letters. Different British government bureaucratic investigations were carried out to ascertain what they actually said and were meant to say and could come up with no firm conclusions. All these scholars and experts assumed the correspondence had been drafted by competent people and that its phrases made sense. They didn't.

Historian Elie Kedourie established that McMahon, who did not speak or write Arabic fluently, had entrusted the translation to his assistant, Ronald Storrs, who did write and speak Arabic. More precisely, Storrs *thought* he did. Storrs was that familiar figure—the criminally incompetent bungler who is also charming and endlessly resourceful at covering up his own catastrophic foul-ups.

Kedourie established that, as drafted and translated into Arabic, the phrases in McMahon and Storrs's correspondence that supposedly ceded control of Palestine to the Arabs and Sherif Hussein made no grammatical or geographical sense. Storrs simply could not write Arabic properly. The original correspondence clearly never intended to cede control of Palestine to the Arabs. The conduct of all British government ministers over the following years makes clear that none of them ever thought for a second that any such commitment had been made on their behalf.

Sykes-Picot as a grand betrayal may be fiction, but it still makes a great narrative for those who would justify Arab anti-Western or anti-Israel sentiments.

Wingate's Bible-based tactical doctrine appealed to the imagination of a young generation of Jews raised as farmers and shaped by their secular, visionary, pioneering parents to view the Bible as a practical guide to the land around them and to reject the old Jewish tradition of sedentary intellectual religious scholarship. Over the next forty years, leading Israeli generals like Dayan, Yigael Yadin, and Chaim Herzog would emphasize the importance of taking practical military lessons from the Bible.

The true story of Israel's creation

After World War II ended in 1945, the British bottled up thousands of Holocaust survivors behind barbed wire in new camps, mostly in Cyprus, to prevent them emigrating to Palestine, where they feared their presence would set off a revolution by the Arab majority.

From 1945 to 1947 a fierce guerrilla revolt by two Palestinian Jewish groups—the Irgun Zvai Leumi, or National Military Organization, led by Menachem Begin; and the Lehi, or Fighters for the Freedom of Israel, led by Yitzhak Shamir—forced the British to give up their Mandate. The new United Nations voted to approve the creation of two new states in the Palestine Mandate area: one Jewish, one Arab. The Jewish community leaders accepted the UN plan; the Palestinian Arab leaders, following the lead of Mufti Haj Amin al-Husseini, did not.

Through the 1930s, Husseini had succeeded in making the fight against the Jewish settlement in Palestine an Arab priority. After the British withdrawal from Israel in

He Screwed up the Middle East, but He Might Still Save the World

In 2007, the body of Sir Mark Sykes was exhumed from its lead-lined coffin in Paris and viable pathogens of the 1919 Spanish flu pandemic virus were extracted. Scientists hope the virus may help them produce a vaccine against the threat of an Asian flu pandemic.

spring 1948, the armies of all the neighboring Arab states invaded, determined to extinguish the infant Jewish state. The Israelis never realized that by driving out the British occupiers they would leave themselves alone to fight a desperate war of survival.

Enter Ben-Gurion

The Israelis had no tanks or air force worth the name, they were massively outnumbered, and their Palestinian Arab countrymen were positioned to control key international roads and lines of communication. But the Israelis did have one secret weapon none of their enemies could match: David Ben-Gurion.

Ben-Gurion had been the dominant figure in Palestinian politics for a quarter century, but British policymakers and even prominent British Jews completely underestimated him. They far preferred the sleek, gracious, always impeccably dressed Chaim Weizmann and wrote off Ben-Gurion as a sloppily dressed, labor movement professional politician.

But Weizmann had no sense of government or strategy. As a war leader, he would have been useless. Ben-Gurion, unlike Weizmann, had come up in politics the hard way. First he had been an organizer of the Palestinian Jewish labor movement. Then he organized the main labor left-of-center political party in Jewish Palestine. By 1933, he was already the prime minister in all but name of Jewish Palestine—a position he would hold for most of the next thirty years. In 1940, he was in London through the worst of the Luftwaffe blitz, and studying Churchill's charismatic war leadership served him well.

In 1947, Ben-Gurion alone recognized that the Jews needed to create and equip a full-scale modern army to fight off invasions from the neighboring Arab states. His careful planning proved crucial in providing his people the weapons they needed to escape annihilation. But while he was a great wartime political leader, he was a military amateur of the worst sort.

Like his hero Winston Churchill in Britain during World War II, Ben-Gurion meddled in operational details all the time, got lots of them wrong, and ordered unrealistic and unsuccessful military operations against the advice of his best military commanders. Worst of all, he listened to the supposed "expertise" of American military adventurer Colonel Mickey Marcus, who, though a professional, was no more gifted a strategist or tactician than Ben-Gurion. Marcus's follies led to the worst defeat in Israel's history: the third frontal assault of the Arab Legion's fortress of Latrun.

Chapter 3

THE MESS IN MESOPOTAMIA

How many Americans know that Iraq was a constitutional monarchy for thirty-three years (1925–1958) and an independent democracy for twenty-six years? Or that during that time, democratically elected governments waged an internal war of effective genocide against their own Assyrian communities, repeatedly permitted looting and pogroms against their ancient Jewish communities, and operated secret police forces and torture chambers simultaneously with free and fair elections?

The British rule over Iraq after World War I wasn't a golden age either. The British imported Indian troops to crush a widespread Shiite-led uprising in 1920; tens of thousands died. They prevented the international community from protecting Assyrians from slaughter in 1932–1933. And the democratic Iraqi government bombed defenseless women and children in the villages of rebellious Arab troops.

Iraq as its own separate country was the brainchild of Winston Churchill when he was Britain's colonial overlord after World War I. Churchill quickly came to regret his creation, made at the urging of romantic and mentally unbalanced British Arabophiles like T. E. Lawrence. In World War II, the Iraqi army rose with eagerness to stab Britain in the back and join Nazi Germany. It was Jewish Palestine, later

Guess what?

- Iraq was a democracy for twenty-six years. And it didn't work.

- The Shiites of Iraq twice have led a ferocious nationalist uprising against an English-speaking superpower that wanted to bring Western-style democracy to their country.

- The Israelis helped block a Nazi takeover of Iraq before there was even an Israel.

Israel, that proved the one loyal force to Britain and the Allies in the Middle East. The reconquest of Iraq was launched with scratch forces boldly striking east across the desert from Jerusalem to Baghdad. All this isn't secret or suppressed history. It's just history most people in the West are unaware of.

Just like today: A bad beginning

An invincible English-speaking nation liberates the ancient territories of Mesopotamia from a notoriously vicious and brutal dictatorship. Its soldiers are first welcomed as liberators and the administrators of the occupying power confidently set up new, enlightened systems of Western constitutional and democratic government. But their plans are derailed by a ferocious popular revolt that kills thousands of the liberating power's soldiers, and tens of thousands of native inhabitants die too as the violence rages.

Iraq after 2003? Of course. But it was also Iraq under the British in 1920. In 1920, however, the revolt against the occupying power did not come primarily from Sunni Muslims in the center of the country but from Shiite Muslims in the south.

Troops of the British-controlled Indian Army savagely crushed the uprising. The cost was high. William L. Cleveland, a serious and balanced American authority, puts the death toll at 460 British soldiers and 10,000 Iraqis, mostly Shiites. Later Iraqi estimates put the death toll much higher.

British policy was to act ruthlessly and on a widespread scale after such serious revolts, and the Shiites were certainly cowed. In fact, the Shiites of southern Iraq remained the most cautious and politically quiescent of all the communities in Iraq until Saddam Hussein was toppled and the activist influence of the Islamic Revolution in neighboring Iran finally started to take hold among them.

PC Myth: Democracy Will Bring Peace

Americans like to think all people are the same regardless of their history, their political views, and where they live. The American experience of absorbing waves of immigrants from every corner of the word has led them to think like that. Politically correct politicians and journalists will accuse you of bigotry if you suggest that some people are not quite wired for liberal democracy the way Americans are.

But it took the American people 220 years of development and a revolutionary war just to reach the point of universal white male adult suffrage in the 1820s. And not even forty years after that, American democracy split in two and fought the most bloody civil war the Western world had ever seen. It is quite a stretch to assume that nations lacking the advantage of hundreds of years' (mostly) peaceful legal and constitutional development can easily make the same leap that took us so long. Some stripes of multiculturalists—or, alternatively, some stripes of neoconservatives—like to dismiss the importance of our intellectual and religious heritage. Our philosophy of governance comes from ancient Greece, ancient Rome, and England. Our morality and culture come from Judaism and Christianity. It is a relativist folly to claim that these heritages don't matter.

Democracy, as Winston Churchill famously said, is the worst form of government imaginable, except for all the other ones that have been tried. In other words, it isn't perfect, but it's a lot preferable to the alternatives. But you can't impose it on other countries from the outside. Democracy needs a certain foundation. That foundation does not exist in the deserts of Mesopotamia.

The problem is not that Iraq and its Middle East neighbors are ungovernable—it's that U.S. policymakers never bothered to study the only stable and

continued on next page

continued from previous page

successful form of government the Middle East ever knew: the Ottoman Empire.

Bush administration policymakers made one stupid, idealistic liberal mistake after another in Iraq: they never put enough troops in the country to maintain basic law and order, they disbanded the one force that could peacefully hold Iraq together—its army—and they put their trust in an exiled charlatan politician and convicted criminal about whom their own diplomats and intelligent service had correctly warned them.

When Ahmed Chalabi proved a bust, U.S. policymakers created a ridiculous constitution that couldn't possibly work and that had no connection with the real political experience of ordinary Iraqis. They assumed that free elections would produce a moderate, reasonable parliament that would act quickly to set up a powerful government. They assumed the already powerful and uncompromising militias wouldn't control the main political factions in the parliament. They assumed that political groups with no experience of political give-and-take for forty-five years would suddenly sober up and practice it. No real conservative would have fallen for these delusions for a second.

The Shiite Revolt had lasting consequences on the way the British shaped Iraq. Although the Shiites were already by far the majority population in the country, the British kept them out in the political cold for the next thirty-eight years, up to 1958. The political elite in the corrupt and creaky but recognizably democratic political system in Baghdad were all Sunni Muslims, mainly from the center and north of the country. More important, so were the dominant officer corps of the new Iraqi army

The British also encouraged the new Sunni Muslim elite they favored to think in pan-Arab terms. Iraq eventually joined the new Arab League.

The British thought they could establish themselves as the friends of the Arabs and so undermine their traditional rivals, the French, in the region. They never grasped that Arabs throughout the Middle East hated the Brits more than they did the French—the British had taken control of far more territory and far larger populations. In 1958, it was the Sunni officer corps, nurtured and protected by the British for so long, who finally kicked them out of Iraq. Sunni Muslim control of the nation and its oil wealth lasted another forty-five years until the U.S. Army swept through the country and a new generation of ignorant Western policymakers decided they knew how to remake the country in their own image.

Democracy in Iraq: 1925–1958

Completely absent from the supposedly competent, learned, and sophisticated U.S. media in the fateful months before the U.S. invasion of Iraq in March 2003 was any reference, let alone serious discussion, of what had happened when Iraq last tried democracy. Democracy wasn't a political antibiotic guaranteed to cure Iraqis of all their woes. They had enjoyed what were supposed to be the blessings of a constitutional democracy, freedom of speech, an independent judiciary, a free press, free democratic elections, and an elected parliament for more than a quarter of a century—and the results hadn't been pretty.

What happened in the 1930s when Britain proclaimed Iraq independent under its own rulers (with British troops and guidance remaining, of course)? Exactly the same thing that happened after the December 2005 Iraqi elections that elected the wonderful Iraqi parliament and parties we see today: terrible cross-community massacres and civil war, with the official army enthusiastically participating.

In 1933, right after Britain granted Iraq titular independence, the Iraqi army under Kurdish general Bakr Sidqi launched a massive pogrom against the Christian Assyrian community in northern Iraq, slaughtering many thousands of them. So frightful were the killings that there was a serious move in the League of Nations to try to rescind full Iraqi independence, but it was blocked by Iraq's British protectors.

The political and military history of Iraqi "democracy" under British "guidance" is mind-numbing: it is a bewildering series of intrigues, coups, treacheries, revolts, and the crushing of one tribe after another with brutal military force.

On October 29, 1936, the first military coup in the Arab world took place in Iraq when General Sidqi overthrew the government of the day. In June 1941, British forces in Iraq who had just foiled another coup planning to ally Iraq with the Nazi-Axis side stood back passively while frustrated young Iraqi army officers led their forces to kill hundreds of Iraqi Jews and despoil their community.

Repeated Arab tribal rebellions were crushed by the British-supported regimes during this period with the utmost severity. The British, it should be remembered, ruled Iraq directly for fourteen years, from their military conquest in 1918 to 1932. And they remained the real power in the country behind a succession of puppet governments for the next twenty-six years until 1958.

But in all that time, there was also a secret police. There were torture chambers. There was the crushing and despoiling of minorities. And there were the unpredictable terrors of the Baghdad mob. It took this level of brutality to maintain in Iraq the government the British favored.

A Jewish base for the Allies

In 1941, the Iraqi army, which the British had raised themselves, revolted against the British and kicked them out at the height of World War II. The only loyal ally they could find anywhere in the Middle East was the Jewish community in Palestine, or the Yishuv.

General Erwin Rommel was running rings around the British in the Libyan desert at the time and was threatening Egypt. This left the British, already stretched thin, with almost no forces left to reclaim Iraq. The Arab Legion, which had been lovingly grown for two decades to serve as the main reliable Arab army loyal to the British and to enforce their will throughout the Middle East, semi-rebelled and announced they would not march against their own brethren.

At that moment, Churchill's hinge of fate was swinging wide. If Adolf Hitler had not been so stupid as to send his elite paratroops and other airborne units to be decimated during their conquest of Crete, he could simply have flown enough of them into Iraq to wipe the floor with whatever belated forces the British could scrape together. At that moment, before the Nazi invasion of the Soviet Union, the Luftwaffe easily had the capability to do the job.

But what crucially turned the tide in the British favor was not the Arab Legion of Transjordan and the Sunni-led Iraqi army in which they had

Political Scientists and Idealistic Dreamers Gone Wild

"Iraq needs to be liberated—liberated from big plans. Every time people mentioned it in the last few years, it was to connect it to big ideas: the war against WMD, solving the Arab-Israeli conflict, more recently the war against terrorism and a model of democracy. That's why all these mistakes are made. They're made because Iraq is always in someone's mind the first step to something else."

Ghassan Salamé, political advisor to assassinated United Nations special envoy Sergio Vieira de Mello, quoted in *The Assassins' Gate* by George Packer

lavished so much investment and pride. It was half a million troublemakers they had grown heartily sick of: the Jewish community of Palestine. The British were able to muster a hastily assembled force of their own reserve troops, Arab Legion forces, and Jewish Palestinian volunteers. Because its strategic target was the vital Habbaniyah air base outside Baghdad, it was called Habforce.

How Iraq's Last Democracy Ended

"The regent's sex was first cut off, and then his arms and legs; they were thrown to groups of young men, who ran off waving these members with joyful shouts. By the time the procession reached the ministry of defense on the other side of the river, the body was no more than a bruised and mutilated trunk....What was left of the regent's body that evening was soaked with petrol and set on fire, the brunt remains being thrown into the Tigris."

Elie Kedourie, *Arabic Political Memoirs*

Their column of only six thousand men struck out across the desert from Palestine against apparently impossible odds. The hastily organized light armor/ mobile infantry force was enormously outnumbered by the Iraqi army, now openly Britain's enemy and Hitler's ally. In brief but heavy fighting, Habforce turned the tide. The British reestablished themselves over Iraq. But it had been a close-run thing. It was the nearest the Nazis ever got to seizing control of the oil wealth of the Middle East.

After the Brits put down the 1941 rebellion, the peace didn't last much longer. Even the British Empire could not forever keep the Hashemites on the fictional throne in Baghdad. On July 14, 1958, a military coup toppled the monarchy. Twenty-four-year-old King Faisal II, along with his grandmother, aunt, and uncle, were slaughtered in exceptionally grisly circumstances. First they were machine-gunned by one of the officers carrying out the coup, who later said he was in a "state of madness" when he fired the fatal shots. Then the body of the young king was beheaded. The body of the regent, Crown Prince Abdullah, was then mutilated by a Baghdad mob.

The brutal massacre—on par with the Bolsheviks' slaughter of the czar's family—ended a twenty-six-year era of constitutional democracy in an independent Iraq.

Yet in the months immediately before and after the 2003 U.S. invasion of Iraq, the restoration of a Hashemite monarchy to Iraq was actually seriously propounded in American intellectual journals and was favored by some of the most influential and powerful policymakers in the U.S. government.

No one shed any tears for the Iraqi Hashemites once they were dead and gone. Colonel Abd al-Karim Qasim, who led the military coup that toppled Faisal II, was a widely popular, even beloved figure who was fondly remembered long after he was deposed in a another coup and then executed himself.

Where America went wrong

The fevered Left can cry as loud and as long as it wishes, but no sensible person will believe that the Bush administration invaded Iraq to enrich the oil companies or to distract Americans from other administration shortcomings. U.S. policymakers were entirely sincere in their belief that they could and would bring stable, pro-Western democracy to Iraq following the toppling of Saddam Hussein in March 2003.

But the road to hell is indeed paved with good intentions. The road to Baghdad was overlaid with a naïve and overly charitable view of the influential groups in Iraq. The Bush administration's plan to quickly establish democracy in Iraq stumbled badly because they vastly underestimated the intransigent, unsophisticated, and anti-Western nature of the competing communities.

In 2003 the United States put only a quarter to one-fifth of the land forces into Iraq that were needed to preserve law and order and prevent an immediate collapse into anarchy. Disbanding Saddam's feared army structure was another mistake resulting from misplaced humanitarianism. There was no other force to fill the gap on short notice, and many of Saddam's former officers became the heart of the new Sunni insurgency that rapidly developed. Washington policymakers obsessed about crafting an "ideal" and "balanced" constitution for Iraq and a ponderous machinery of popular elections and parliamentary procedures while they ignored the basic issues of producing enough food, fuel, gasoline, and other economic necessities and guaranteeing a sufficient climate of law and order. They thought the 60 percent Shiite community could rapidly be co-opted either by charlatans like Ahmed Chalabi, who never commanded any significant popular following, or religious leaders like Grand Ayatollah Ali al-Sistani, who played Washington from the start. They never dreamed that Iraq's Shiites, spearheaded by rapidly organizing new militias, could develop an agenda of their own—one contrary to U.S. interests.

Why Western governance doesn't work there

The answer to this question—which seems to have escaped such prominent writers as Thomas Friedman and Charles Krauthammer—was that Iraq isn't the United States, or anything like it. Democracy could work in Germany and Italy after World War II because, for three quarters of a century from the 1860s onward, there had been a free press, free parliaments (even if their powers were somewhat limited), and free elections in those countries before the Fascist takeovers of the 1920s and 1930s. To a lesser but still significant degree, the same was true in Japan following the Meiji Restoration of 1869 all the way to the military assassinations and effective takeover of the 1930s.

But as we have seen, during the forty years of British presence from 1918 (and the twenty-six years of constitutional democracy from 1932 to 1958) the reality in Iraq was tribal rivalries, military coups, secret police, and torture chambers. And in the thirty-five years of the Second Ba'ath Republic from 1968 to 2003, Iraq was a totalitarian state of the most extreme sort. Before the British occupation in 1918, there had never been the slightest semblance of modern political culture in Iraq—in striking contrast, for example, to Egypt.

The Iraqi conception of politics was the same merciless, winner-take-all, kill-or-be-killed, zero-sum game that Lenin summed

A Book You're Not Supposed to Read

The Chatham House Version and other Middle Eastern Studies by Elie Kedourie; Chicago: Ivan R. Dee, 2004.

up as "Who/Whom." You were either "Who"—the subject of the verb, the aggressor, the victimizer—or else you had no choice but "Whom"—the object of the verb, the passive victim helpless to defend himself from whatever the ruler did to him. The contemporary urban equivalent of Lenin's idea—and Iraq's politics—would be "*get* or get *got.*"

This wasn't an American conception of politics. It certainly wasn't a liberal one. But it was the way things had always worked in Iraq.

After Saddam: "Better Tiberius"

A wise old historian once said, "Better Tiberius than a committee." Tiberius was one of the worst tyrants in the history of the Roman Empire, and Saddam Hussein made him look like Mother Teresa. But rule in Baghdad by the "committee" Defense Secretary Donald Rumsfeld installed turned out to be far worse.

Saddam had been the greatest killer in modern Arab history. He had unleashed two major wars of aggression, attacking Iran and swallowing Kuwait. He had inflicted monstrous atrocities on his own people. The only thing he wasn't guilty of was the crime that precipitated the 2003 U.S. invasion that finally took him down—funding or other involvement in the planning of the September 11 attacks. But Iraq and the Middle East were vastly more dangerous places after he fell than they were during his last twelve years of power.

The original assessment by President George H. W. Bush, Secretary of State James A. Baker, national security advisor Brent Scowcroft, and General Colin Powell—one of the best national security teams in modern U.S. history—to leave Saddam in power in Baghdad was sound. This became very clear after U.S. military forces finally moved into Baghdad for an extended stay in April 2003.

Saddam in power had been an effective block on the Iranians. President Ronald Reagan, Secretary of State George Shultz, and their national security teams had recognized this clearly. They saw that Iran was incomparably the greater long-term threat to the United States—and to Israel for

PC Myth: Democracy Guarantees Human Rights

The Hashemite monarchy and its parliament didn't produce the moderate, civilizing, and restrained influence constitutional monarchies are supposed to encourage. Iraq's Jews, Kurds, Shiites, and many Sunni Muslim tribes all paid the price for "democracy" in a nation that had had no history of constitutional evolution or law. The sweeping confiscation of almost all the property of Iraq's ancient Jewish community (more than 100,000 strong) was actually carried out according to parliamentary and constitutional propriety on a single day in March 1951.

Far from bringing peace, democracy in Iraq guaranteed war. The competing groups in Iraq from 1932 to 1958 saw the democratic process only as a battle through which to seize the institutions of power and then wield them ruthlessly against everyone else. In nearly half a century since the July 14, 1958, coup, nothing has changed.

that matter—after Iraq's potentially catastrophic nuclear potential had been destroyed in the 1981 Israeli air force raid. That was why the Bush team backed Iraq to the hilt in its 1980–1988 war against Iran.

Saddam was the only thing stopping Iran from steadily spreading its influence into Iraq, with its 60 percent Shiite majority population. As long as the Iraq state remained stable and dominated by its Sunni minority, the Iranian Islamic revolutionaries were blocked. So fearsome was Saddam's justly deserved reputation after they were crushed in their 1991 revolt that the Shiite majority of the south would not dare defy him. When old Grand Ayatollah Mohammed Sadiq al-Sadr was murdered almost certainly on Saddam's orders in 1999, there was not a whisper out of the Iraqi Shiite majority. They knew what would happen to them.

But once Saddam was gone, it was a very different story. Donald Rumsfeld froze the State Department, the CIA, and every other part of the U.S. government out of running Iraq. But then he and his top staff didn't bother to do the job themselves.

A large body of young democracy-touting ideologues, none of whom spoke Arabic or had ever lived in, let alone studied, the history of the Arab world, were flown out to the Green Zone: the comfortable, Starbucks-equipped enclave in Baghdad from which U.S. forces ruled. As the Coalition Provisional Authority (CPA), they intended to create a new constitution for Iraq and decide how the country should be ruled. They made the bungling British Empire look competent.

Banking on a bank swindler

Rumsfeld's policymakers bet heavily on a wealthy Shiite Iraqi adventurer and exile who had been convicted years before of massive bank fraud in Jordan. He escaped a long jail sentence only by fleeing the country.

There was not the slightest reason to believe that Ahmed Chalabi and his Iraqi National Congress (INC) were a force in Iraq. The State Department and serious CIA analysts were extremely skeptical of him all along. But their accurate assessments and warnings were ignored by their gung-ho political masters. Yet the assumption that Chalabi was beloved by the Iraqi people, including large numbers in the Sunni-dominated Iraqi army, shored up U.S. war planning from the first. Rumsfeld even wanted to pare the invading U.S. force down from 150,000–180,000 troops to a mere 50,000–60,000 because he was so convinced the Iraqi army wouldn't fight and large elements of it would defect to U.S. forces as soon as they crossed the border.

Of course, that didn't happen. But the delusion that Chalabi and his INC would rapidly become the credible, eagerly pro-American government in Iraq died hard. Eventually the CIA gathered compelling evidence that Chalabi may have been an agent for the Iranians all along, and, at the very least, was a serious security risk. They were convinced that he had leaked confidential codes and information he should never have had to the Iranians. Rumsfeld's lieutenants then cut off their links to him—at least for a time.

Even without Chalabi, the naïve U.S. planners in the Green Zone and their political masters back home weren't too perturbed. They had invaded and occupied Iraq to make it safe for democracy, and make it safe they would. Through 2005, the insurgents inflicted a hail of bomb attacks decimating the new Iraqi police and security forces. The new police forces were undertrained, possessed dubious loyalty, and were incapable of operating independently against insurgent forces.

That's the Way It Is

"Brief as it is, the record of the kingdom of Iraq is full of bloodshed, treason, and rapine and however pitiful its end, we may now say this was implicit in its beginning."

Elie Kedourie, "The Kingdom of Iraq: A Retrospect," in *The Chatham House Version and Other Studies*

Throughout Iraq, real power fell into the hands of local militias, both Sunni and Shiite. During this fateful time, the CPA planners in Baghdad focused on crafting an ideal constitution for Iraq. They might as well have counted the number of angels that could dance on the head of a pin. Without any real government worth the name, Iraqis went hungry, weren't paid, lacked electricity for long parts of the day, and didn't even have enough gasoline in the country with the second largest and most accessible reserves of the stuff on earth. Even Saddam started to look good, and that took some doing.

Birth of the Iraqi insurrection

Bush's idealistic advisors, dead set on making Iraq into a nice Western-style democracy, believed Ahmed Chalabi when he said he would be hugely popular and that the U.S. Army would be greeted as liberators.

It never happened. Within twenty-three days of the fall of Baghdad on April 9, 2003, the great Sunni insurrection against U.S. forces was already up and running. It started on May 1, 2007, the same day President George W. Bush dramatically landed on the nuclear aircraft carrier USS *Abraham Lincoln* and proclaimed "Mission Accomplished." On that day, U.S. soldiers in the Sunni town of Fallujah shot and killed sixteen violent demonstrators who were not carrying firearms.

The dead protesters promptly became martyrs. From Ireland to India, nothing sets mass emotions aflame and whips up widespread popular support like a dozen or more martyrs—people who can be plausibly presented as the tragic victims of the evil occupying power. Combine these inevitable flare-ups with Rumsfeld's insistence on having almost no visible presence on the Iraqi streets, and a violent insurgency should be expected. As Machiavelli taught, making people mad at you is fine as long as they're afraid of you. But making people mad at you without making them afraid of you is the worst mistake in the book. Rumsfeld's Pentagon and their tame CPA made that mistake in spades.

The great anti-American insurrection in Iraq over the next four years succeeded where Saddam Hussein and the most powerful and hitherto successful conventional army in the Arab world had totally failed twice. The Sunni Iraqi insurgents stymied, neutralized, and began to exhaust the U.S. armed forces that had easily wiped out the regular Iraqi army in three weeks.

The Sunni Muslim insurrection in Iraq soon attracted significant international jihadists to its ranks, and over the years they came to make up a significant number of the suicide bomber cadres who inflicted the worst mayhem on Shiite civilians and the new Iraqi armed forces.

But it didn't start that way. Al Qaeda and other such groups did not launch the insurrection in Iraq, were not primarily responsible for its growth, and never made up more than a small minority of its active fighters. By fall 2005, U.S. military intelligence assessments in Iraq had concluded that the insurrection had reached the self-sustaining point. Even if all arms supplies and volunteers from outside the country could be cut off—and, given the paucity of U.S. ground forces in the country, that wasn't remotely possible—the insurgency would continue at exactly the same level it had reached.

The insurgents: Not just a few troublemakers

In August 2003 Iraqi insurgents killed the United Nations envoy to Iraq, Sergio Vieira de Mello, and twenty-one members of his UN staff with an enormous truck bomb that demolished the Canal Hotel in Baghdad. The widely respected de Mello was the highest-ranking UN official to be killed in the course of duty in more than four decades. That same "Black August," Grand Ayatollah Mohamed Baqir al-Hakim, the most senior

PC Myth: We Don't Need the Big, Bad Ba'athists

The Coalition Provisional Authority should have taken control of Saddam's well-disciplined and justly feared army, paying its troops and selecting a useful general from the old regime to lead it. That part should have been easy; Saddam treated his generals like dirt, especially if they served him well and were good at their jobs.

But instead, the hapless L. Paul Bremer, apparently on orders from Rumsfeld and his right-hand men running the Pentagon at the time, dissolved the Iraqi army and issued a de-Ba'athification order eliminating anyone who had served in the Ba'ath Party from any position of official responsibility. That wasn't a conservative way to do things: it was neo-liberal idealism at its most dangerous and stupid.

The de-Ba'athification order also ignored the practice and lessons of General George S. Patton, greatest of all U.S. combat commanders, who got into hot water after World War II by keeping former members of the Nazi Party around to ensure southern Germany didn't collapse into famine and chaos after World War II.

For Patton understood the nature of the totalitarian state: every engineer, doctor, or technocrat worth his salt is forced to join the ruling party just to be allowed to do his job.

De-Ba'athification could have been done with discrimination and success (it would be hard to imagine it being conducted less successfully) if post-occupation investigators had focused solely on secret police killers and top party officials involved with enforcing Saddam's most notorious and bloody initiatives.

Instead, 50,000 to 60,000 men who were the best armed and best trained in Iraq were alienated from the U.S. forces, the CPA, and any Iraqis who threw their lot in with them. And the entire Sunni community in central Iraq was sent the message that after eighty-three years of being top dog, there was going to be no hope for them at the hands of their vengeful Shiite brethren. Bremer and his young staffers in the CPA didn't intend to send them that message. But then, they didn't know anything about Iraq.

Shiite cleric in Iraq, and eighty of his supporters were killed in another devastating car bomb attack.

Naïve U.S. commentators didn't get it. They opined that the attacks were clearly the work of a small minority (true) comprised overwhelmingly of foreigners to Iraq (false). What they didn't realize was that Iraq was rapidly devolving into the "state of nature" described by British polit-

PC Myth: We Don't Need Troops on the Ground

Defense Secretary Donald Rumsfeld, obsessed with the idea that the United States could remain the world's global hyper-power with an army marginally larger than North Korea's, refused to authorize any extra troops or—better by far—police to keep the country calm, safe, and law-abiding during the tumultuous days and weeks after Saddam's fall. When an orgy of rioting predictably erupted across Baghdad, Rumsfeld shrugged it off with the now-famous comment, "Stuff happens."

Wise old Sir Herbert Dowbiggin, the tough British colonial policeman who probed the causes of the 1929 Arab riots in Palestine, could have told Rumsfeld what would happen next.

First, crucial damage was done to Iraq's critical infrastructure, especially its electrical generating capacity and oil production facilities, with monumental impact on the nation's recovery prospects for the following years.

Second, the Iraqi people lost whatever awe they had of the U.S. Army. (The U.S. Army, it should be remembered, flooded its occupation zone in southern Germany and all of Japan with troops after its victories at the end of World War II.)

ical philosopher Thomas Hobbes: a state without effective government, where gangs and terror groups proliferated and killed at will; a state, as Hobbes memorably put it, where life was "poor, nasty, brutish, and short."

The Sunni insurgents were culled primarily from the 20 percent Sunni minority in Iraq that had ruled the roost ever since the British crushed the 1920 Shiite revolt. They saw clearly they had no realistic stake in a "new" Iraq where the Americans were building up the Shiites to be top dog. Because Rumsfeld refused to flood Iraq with American troops to keep law and order, and because CPA head L. Paul Bremer had disbanded the old Iraqi army—which everyone in the country had been justly scared of—anarchy and terrorism ruled. New local militias, Shiite and Sunni alike, started to coalesce to give a semblance of protection to their local neighborhoods.

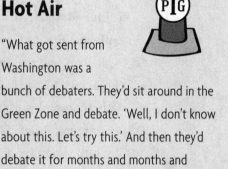

A Lot of Hot Air

"What got sent from Washington was a bunch of debaters. They'd sit around in the Green Zone and debate. 'Well, I don't know about this. Let's try this.' And then they'd debate it for months and months and months and months and nothing would happen."

U.S. military combat veteran and personal injury lawyer **John Smathers** to Rajiv Chandrasekaran

The undermanned and overstretched U.S. forces in Iraq were rapid-movement elite combat units—the best in the world. They were not policemen and they had not been trained as counter-insurgency experts. They responded to attacks and threats as they had been trained, with overwhelming firepower and calling in air strikes when they needed them. That was the way to win conventional wars, but not to win hearts and minds in a counter-insurgency conflict. Innocent people were inevitably killed and their homes destroyed—not because our soldiers were murderers, but because they were soldiers rather than peace-keepers. Every time that happened, it was a huge political gift to the insurgents.

The insurgents also developed a new war-winning weapon that single-handedly transformed the operational dynamics of the war: simple, old-fashioned, booby-trap bombs that earned the fancy name "improvised explosive device," or IED. They employed shaped charges and modern explosives that rendered the Americans' Bradley Fighting Vehicles highly vulnerable. Since September 11, Rumsfeld's Pentagon had been showered with financial support by sympathetic Congresses like no previous Department of Defense or war in U.S. history, but Rumsfeld invested most of it into visionary, science-fiction-type, high-tech wonder systems of the future. There was no money at first to buy simple steel plates to buckle onto the sides and bottoms of U.S. combat vehicles in Iraq. Eventually, hundreds of U.S. soldiers would die or lose their limbs before that oversight was laboriously rectified.

Even after all these bungles, however, the situation could have been reversed if well-intentioned policymakers had been set on winning a guerrilla war rather than instilling a beautiful and pure parliamentary democracy in Iraq. On December 15, 2005, they unveiled their pride and joy—genuinely free and fair parliamentary elections throughout Iraq.

Bombing the Golden Mosque: The point of no return

For nearly three years after invading Iraq, U.S. policymakers imposed radical, romantic, liberal nation-building policies on the hapless country, claiming the plans were either conservative or essential for national security. In truth, the people who came up with the bright ideas and pushed them through were neither conservative in any meaningful sense nor knowledgeable about the region.

But if there was a single moment that could be called the Point of No Return, it was terror master Abu Musab al-Zarqawi's final masterstroke. On February 22, 2006, Sunni Muslim insurgents bombed one of the most sacred shrines in Shiite Islam, the al-Askariya Mosque, or the Golden Mosque, in Samarra.

PC Myth: Democracy Can Solve Iraq's Problems

Turnout in the Iraqi elections of December 2005 was high: 70 percent (a far higher turnout than for most U.S. elections). The Iraqi people expressed their free, democratic will loud and clear, and they voted for...more chaos and civil war.

After nearly three years of escalating terror, suffering, and chaos, the outcome should have been a predictable one: the three main ethnic or religious groups in Iraq—the Shiites of the south, the minority Sunnis of the center, and the Kurds of the north—all voted for their traditional local partisan parties. This was the same pattern seen in any seriously divided society that has suffered civil war or serious sectarian strife (Sri Lanka, Northern Ireland, Bosnia, and Lebanon are a few examples). Many of the factions elected to the new parliament in Baghdad were controlled by or had strong ties to the most implacable terror groups or militias.

Shiites swept the board, winning 62 percent of the vote. Sunnis, despite being one-fifth of the population, won only 8 percent of the seats in the new parliament. The results boosted the Shiites and Kurds backed by U.S. policymakers and left the Sunnis feeling out in the cold, recalling the saying that democracy is two wolves and a sheep deciding what to have for dinner, and liberty is a well-armed lamb. The insurgents became more popular than ever in the Sunni community, and that made them more bold. Their recruiting figures soared, and so did their ability to carry out more terror attacks.

U.S. policymakers had naïvely believed the elections would suck the air out of popular Sunni support for the insurgency. Instead, it only fanned the flames. The rates at which U.S. soldiers, Iraqi security forces, and innocent—mostly Shiite—civilians were killed soared in the months following the elections.

Shiite militias around the country, especially in Baghdad, reacted at once with murderous fury. Hundreds of innocent Sunnis were shot at random or, even worse, dragged off to be tortured. Sunnis reacted by rallying behind the insurgents and other militia groups within their own community.

There was not even an independent Iraqi government yet functioning in Baghdad to pretend it could halt the mayhem. More than two months after the parliamentary elections America's Green Zone bureaucrats were so proud of, the squabbling Iraqi political parties—most of them merely fronts for murderous militia groups—were still far from agreement about a government. And there were still far too few U.S. troops on the ground to guarantee law and order and end the killing.

Tens of thousands died as the waves of tit-for-tat random killings flowed back and forth. Hundreds of thousands of Iraqis fled their homes to find refuge in enclaves run by militias of their own religious tradition. The power of the Sunni insurgents in their own community grew, and in the following months, the scale of terror attacks by Sunnis grew by leaps and bounds.

But the biggest beneficiaries of the al-Askariya bombing and the bloodbaths that followed were the Shiite militias, especially in Baghdad and southern Iraq. It was they, and not the ephemeral Shiite-led governments that U.S. diplomats frantically patched together, who soon came to be the real power in Shiite Iraq.

Shiite militias soon gathered vastly more power than the Sunni insurgents ever had. They had strong ties to all the new Iraqi security forces, which in reality were controlled and run by Shiite senior officers. They also had a powerful influence on the ramshackle new Iraqi governments, including Prime Minister Nouri al-Maliki's. At one time, five of Maliki's cabinet ministers and a bloc of thirty members of the new Iraqi Parliament were loyal to Moqtada al-Sadr, the charismatic—and most anti-American—Shiite militia leader who runs the Mahdi Army. Sadr and his

Mahdi Army remained the real power in the Shiite stronghold of Sadr City within Baghdad. They are at the heart of a tight network of Shiite militias across the southern half of the country.

It isn't a civil war; it's a splinter war

For all of 2006 and most of 2007, President Bush and his spokesmen labored to deny the obvious: a full-fledged civil war was already raging in Iraq.

In one sense, all the president's men were telling the truth. Following the February 22, 2006, bombing of the Golden Mosque in Samarra, it wasn't a civil war that was raging in Iraq. It was something far worse: a splinter war.

A Book You're Not Supposed to Read

American mainstream historians have paid virtually no attention to the Anglo-Jewish reconquest of Iraq in 1941. An exception is Howard M. Sachar's superb *Europe Leaves the Middle East: 1936–1954*, New York: Allen Lane Publishers, 1974.

Sachar combines high scholarship with a vivid, descriptive writing style that makes the events he describes come crackling to life. His book integrates the different military campaigns during World War II and gives a rare and excellent overview.

A civil war pits the government against a faction trying to take power for itself. A splinter war occurs when a central government collapses completely and lots of little militias and local groups immediately start squabbling and killing each other.

Splinter wars are the norm in Thomas Hobbes's "state of nature." They often kill more innocents than civil wars do, because killing is random and done by lots of different groups and because public services like electricity and hospitals tend to collapse.

In April 2006 I coined another phrase to describe the kind of war the U.S. armed forces were forced to deal with in Iraq: a war according to Belfast Rules or Beirut Rules.

These are the rules that apply when national armies, occupying forces, or international peacekeepers try to maintain order and security and try

PC Myth: Kill Zarqawi and We Win

On June 7, 2006, Abu Musab al-Zarqawi was killed by a precision U.S. air strike on a supposed safe house where he was plotting mayhem at the time. His killing was a triumph for the hard-pressed U.S. and Iraqi security forces and eliminated al Qaeda's outstanding leader in Iraq, a man more responsible than any other for the extreme savagery of the Sunni insurgency there. Yet the year after his death saw no reduction in the insurgency's capabilities to carry out lethal bombings against Shiite civilians. There were important reasons why this was so.

Zarqawi was a figure of the kind often found in anti-colonial and guerrilla wars of the past century. He was a merciless, brutal fanatic who was also a tactical genius and a superb operational commander. But his indiscriminate killing and his bloodlust toward fellow Muslims, especially Shiites, threatened to isolate the insurgency by mobilizing the Shiite majority in Iraq, which has three times the population of the Sunnis. Zarqawi also prioritized attacks on U.S. forces in Iraq, a strategic policy that hastened his own demise.

Zarqawi's death immediately made headlines around the world. But the level of attrition inflicted on U.S. forces in Iraq by Sunni insurgents remained high, and the insurgents were able to keep up the casualty rate.

Why did the tactical U.S. successes against al Qaeda within Iraq fail to quell the insurgency? Part of the answer is that al Qaeda and its allies had already succeeded in pulverizing the credibility of Iraq's three democratically elected governments by the time U.S. forces could make real inroads against them.

The U.S. obsession with ambitious, cumbersome constitutional processes distracted American planners from being able to focus on the primary issues of restoring electricity and running water and having enough reliable U.S. and

continued on next page

continued from previous page

allied troops to ensure law and order. As a result, none of the three civilian governments of Iraq enjoyed any grassroots credibility. They were unable to deliver basic protection or reliable services to a significant portion of the population.

Even in supposedly peaceful Shiite majority provinces across southern Iraq, the government forces operate in alliance with—or at the sufferance of—a patchwork of Shiite militias that they do not control.

Killing Zarqawi didn't come near to ending the war because al Qaeda was never the only, or even the main, arm of the Sunni resistance. By the time Zarqawi was killed, he was first among equals in a shifting coalition of anti-American Sunni militia groups. And when Zarqawi succeeded in provoking an overwhelming Shiite reaction after the al-Askariya bombing, he achieved his ultimate strategic goal of making Iraq ungovernable through the U.S.-guided democratic political process. It was tempting to think that the Iraqi people would be grateful we had freed them of their brutal dictator and that democracy and the promise of a brighter future would overwhelm their bitterness and tribalism, but such hopeful dreams "misoverestimated" the Iraqi people.

U.S. grand strategy in Iraq, in its obsession with Zarqawi and al Qaeda, never confronted the messy religious and ethnic political and paramilitary realities of the country. President George W. Bush, Vice President Dick Cheney, and Defense Secretary Donald Rumsfeld remained convinced that once Zarqawi was hunted down and killed and al Qaeda's operational command structure was smashed, then the Sunni insurgency would evaporate and peaceful, democratic political processes would at last triumph in Iraq.

But it did not happen that way.

to prevent the massacre of thousands of people when the central government has totally broken down. Beirut and Belfast rules apply when sectarian-based militias hold power in nations that have already splintered or fragmented into conditions of civil war. They are what U.S. soldiers now face in Baghdad.

Why the surge couldn't tame Baghdad

There were many reasons why the much heralded 2007 "surge" of U.S. troops in Iraq, focused on Baghdad, could never have worked.

During the first few months of the surge, militia killings in Baghdad fell significantly. But at the same time, Baghdad fell ever more tightly under the control of a web of violent Shiite militias while the Shiite-dominated national government was simultaneously powerless to stop it and passively complicit in the process. And in the summer of 2007, even as violence was dropping rapidly in Anbar Province, it was rising again to its old levels in Baghdad.

The surge also demonstrated the futility of those armchair strategists and "warrior" pundits and politicians back in the United States who had talked so glibly about "unleashing" the U.S. armed forces to bring security to Baghdad.

For neither the American armed forces nor the ramshackle Iraqi parliamentary-democratic system that U.S. authorities imposed on Iraq could bring peace, prosperity, security, or basic guaranteed daily services to the Iraqi capital. For these services, the people of Baghdad in 2006 and 2007 came to rely on their neighborhood militias. Like the mafia in crime-ridden cities of old, the Shiite militias became the real government of the Iraqi capital.

And when militia forces are deeply rooted in their own local community strongholds and are seen by enough of their inhabitants as the community's defenders, war against them is seen as war against the entire community.

That is the nightmare scenario U.S. armed forces were facing in Baghdad in the closing months of 2007 when forced to fight a campaign of annihilation or repression against the dominant Shiite militias in Baghdad.

In theory, by busting up militias, U.S. soldiers would be carrying out the work of the democratic government of Iraq, and thus doing the people's will. In the people's eyes, however, a foreign occupying force was warring against the only institutions holding their communities together.

The more U.S. firepower and military force used against the militias—and the more civilian casualties concomitantly inflicted—the more the Shiite population of Baghdad would become bitterly opposed to the U.S. presence. As the conflict escalated, U.S military forces would become embattled and besieged. The Iraqi government—a government in little more than name—at best would try to help ineffectually, and at worst could easily become a conduit for intelligence and sabotage on behalf of the Shiite militias.

The U.S. Army historically has had little experience of the complexities, viciousness, and enormous casualties that full-scale street fighting in an urban environment can generate. Americans should pray they never have to learn.

Chapter 4

THE TRUTH ABOUT ISLAM
RADICAL ISLAM ISN'T ANCIENT
(WHICH MAKES IT MORE DANGEROUS)

The Muslim nations of the Middle East took an irrevocable turn toward radical Islam not in the tenth century, not after the fall of Baghdad to the Mongols in the thirteenth century, but in 1979. The key event was Ayatollah Ruhullah Khomeini's Islamic Revolution in Iran and his successful defiance of the United States. Two other events fueled the trend. Since 1973, the Saudi monarchy had been making such huge oil profits that it could afford to export radical versions of its own fundamentalist Wahhabi version of Islam throughout South and Southeast Asia. And also in 1979, the Soviet invasion of Afghanistan inspired successive U.S. administrations, Democratic and Republican alike, to fund Islamist mujahedin guerrillas in their defiance of the Red Army.

Guess what?

- Radical Islamist terror as we know it is only thirty years old.

- Jimmy Carter's handling of the Iranian hostage crisis aided the rise of radical Islam.

The wisdom of Prince Turki

The new, radical, and un-Islamic nature of the modern wave of Islamist terror was explained in August 2005 by Prince Turki al-Faisal, the former head of Saudi intelligence.

Turki, who had served for almost four years the kingdom's ambassador to Britain, told a workshop in London that the extreme Islamist terrorists were inspired by non-Islamic cult psychology. He argued that the real nature of terrorist organizations like al Qaeda was not Islamic, but rather a cult psychology that had borrowed Islamic language to propagate deranged messages and justify its actions.

"This terrorism is not based on Islam, but is a perverted cult ideology. Its followers have absented themselves from normal society and from the family, and placed themselves outside of reality to fulfill fantasies that have nothing to do with the real world," Turki said. "It is a terrorist cult, rather than a classic terrorist organization like the IRA or ETA."

His comments were not original ones. Many pundits and Islamic scholars have made similar points. They have noted that, far from being any kind of logical extension of traditional Islam, the kind of nihilistic violence and revolution advocated by Osama bin Laden and others is akin to the revolutionary utopianism of Bolshevism and the Russian and Chinese revolutions. Except this time, it is wrapped in the imagery of one of the world's great, ancient, monotheistic religions, and among its goals are the overthrow of secular and moderate traditional Muslim governments and the establishment of an idealized super-powerful caliphate over the entire Muslim world.

The kind of people attracted by this message, as was the case with Marxism, are not the actual poor and suffering, who are overwhelmingly preoccupied with making ends meet and securing better lives for themselves and their families. They are the displaced, rootless intellectuals, the "superfluous men" described by the great nineteenth-century Russian novelist Fyodor Dostoevsky as being the driving force of the revolutionary movement.

British security service MI5 certainly shares Prince Turki's assessment. Their psychological profiles have predicted that dangerous, alienated revolutionaries were more likely to be recruited from middle-class university backgrounds than from mean slums.

But as the July 7, 2005, suicide bombings in London showed, the British security services, unlike their French, Russian, and Israeli counterparts, badly underestimated the potential scale of the problem. After the discovery that British-born Muslims of Pakistani descent had set off the bombs that killed fifty-six people and wounded seven hundred more, the British security services multiplied their estimate of the number of people in Britain capable of carrying out such attacks by a factor of one hundred: from thirty to three thousand.

Prince Turki's assessment revealed that the Saudi government correctly understood the complex and serious nature of the problem. They recognized that for the war against the Islamists to be won, they must first be isolated from the mainstream of the Islamic world.

The cycles of Arab history

Looking at the Middle East in the first decade of the twenty-first century, it's easy to imagine that the great driving force radicalizing the region and turning it against the West is and always was the religion of Islam. It is certainly the case, as the mega-terrorist attacks of September 11 so awfully confirmed, that a fanatical anti-American, anti-Western, and anti-Israeli dynamic seethed through the region, and that extreme Islam had become its driving force. But this was an exceptionally late development. What is extraordinary about Middle East history through the first three-quarters of the twentieth century is not the dynamic power of Islam but its almost total absence.

Islam was nonexistent as a motivating force for the Muslim peoples of the Middle East through both world wars. The sultan-caliphs in Constantinople called upon Muslims of the world to rise against the British Empire. None of them did. The British imagined that if they could get Sherif Hussein of Mecca, the guardian of the most sacred Islamic holy places, whose line of descent went back to the prophet Mohammad himself, on their side, they would be able to play the Muslim or jihad card against the Ottomans. That didn't work either.

The only Arab leader who stood strong and independent through World War I was Abdulaziz ibn Saud. And while he championed a more austere and traditional form of desert Islam, he appealed only to his own tribesmen and to the population of the Hejaz coastal region of Arabia who had had their fill of old Sherif Hussein. Ibn Saud never dreamed of playing any jihad holy war card against the British and the French. He wasn't that stupid.

After World War I, the parliamentary democracies of Britain and France, the nations that had won the Great War, seemed to the peoples of the Middle East to offer the best path to the restoration of their national independence, eventual prosperity, and national dignity. The charismatic example and success of Mustafa Kemal Ataturk in neighboring Turkey also suggested this was the way to go. But then, in the 1930s, the rise of Fascist Italy and Nazi Germany seemed to humble the exhausted parliamentary democracies. Arab political leaders were far from unique in being impressed by the Fascists and the Nazis. The military leaders in many Latin American countries, in Japan, and even Chiang Kai-shek in China made the same mistake.

Gamal Abdel Nasser's success in defying Britain and France with Soviet support in the 1956 Suez crisis convinced millions of people across the region that Arab socialism modeled on and backed by the Soviet Union was the way to go. Nasser's repeated failures and humiliation with Syria, in Yemen, and repeatedly at the hands of the Israelis in the 1960s helped deflate that idea. Stable Ba'ath socialist regimes weren't established in Iraq and Syria until 1968 and 1970, respectively. But they proved less than attractive to neighboring countries.

This Arab socialist cycle backed by the Soviets lasted about thirty years—from the establishment of the State of Israel to the start of the Islamic Revolution in Iran in 1978. Since then, the main focus for the frustrations, aspirations, and ambitions of the Arab world has been fundamentalist Islamism. This hasn't had a steady record of failure or success either. The early prestige of Ayatollah Khomeini and his followers in Iran was dented profoundly by their repeated military defeats at the hands of the Iraqi army during the Iran-Iraq War. At least half a million Iranian soldiers, many of them just teenagers or even younger, died in crazed and futile suicide attacks. The actual figure may even be far higher. But at the same time, a new generation of young Islamists was winning credit across the Arab world, especially in traditional societies like Saudi Arabia, for their bravery and effectiveness in fighting the Soviet Red Army in Afghanistan. Ironically, the government of President Ronald Reagan was their most important supporter and supplier.

When Saddam Hussein conquered Kuwait and for six months defied the United States and its allies in 1990–1991, he briefly enjoyed the kind of acclaim as a popular warrior-hero that Nasser had enjoyed in the years after Suez. But it didn't last. Saddam was never able to undermine or destabilize Arab governments around the region the way Nasser had managed to do after Suez. On the contrary, not only Saudi Arabia and Egypt, but even Syria rallied to the United States to contain him. They had good reason to be scared of him. So Saddam's pan-Arab and quasi-Muslim rhetoric, like that of so many before him, fell flat.

Osama bin Laden did a lot better than that when his success in killing three thousand Americans in a single day, mauling the Pentagon, and destroying the World Trade Cen-

What's a Wahhabi?

Wahhabism began two hundred years ago as a reform movement to rid Islamic societies of supposedly lax cultural practices and interpretations that had built up over the centuries. Most Wahhabis live in Saudi Arabia, and almost all Muslims in Mecca and Medina are Wahhabis.

ter made him a popular hero across the Arab world. All of a sudden, extreme Islamism looked like a heroic success story again. Since then, U.S. bungles in Iraq and Israeli missteps with the Palestinians have seen Hamas seize power in Gaza and Islamist guerrillas continue to terrorize Iraq.

The threat posed by extremist Islam and its proliferating groups is very real and shouldn't be discounted. Our planet's last hundred years show us clearly that peaceful nations sometimes discount fringe radicals at their own peril. Nobody besides the czars took seriously the obscure, feuding, revolutionary adherents of Karl Marx in Russia before World War I. But then the Soviet Union was created and the Communist fringe controlled the largest nation on earth. In 1920, its armies swept west and until they were stopped by the Poles in the Battle of the Vistula River looked ready to turn Germany Communist and then dominate the rest of Europe. Similarly, in 1923 and for years later, Adolf Hitler seemed like nothing more than a bad joke to the governments of the world, including that of his own country. No one dreamed he would become the greatest continental conqueror since Napoleon and the most merciless killer since Genghis Khan.

Bin Laden's al Qaeda and its related groups should be seen in this light. If they can be contained, and if the national governments committed to eradicating them are not undermined, the prospects for marginalizing them remain excellent. But that situation can rapidly change. As it is, the Bush administration's fateful enthusiasm for spreading Western-style democracy as rapidly and completely as possible across the Middle East was arguably a bungle at least as fateful as Eisenhower rescuing Nasser in 1956 or Jimmy Carter undermining the shah in 1977.

The bottom line is that the Arab Middle East went through two full political cycles after the fall of the Ottoman Empire. The first, from 1917 to around 1950, saw it try on liberal parliamentary democracy. When that didn't fit, and when the main semi-parliamentary states of Egypt, Syria, and Iraq failed to eradicate Israel in the 1947–1948 war, the second thirty-year cycle began. That was the cycle of revolutionary Arab socialism backed by the Soviet Union. The Islamic Revolution in Iran and the Soviet invasion of Afghanistan put paid to that and launched the third cycle: the period of extreme Islamic fundamentalism. This appeared to be very much on the retreat until September 11, 2001, until bin Laden's attacks and America's long, painful occupation of Iraq rejuvenated it.

The Middle East gets religion: 1977–1980

If you examine all the conflicts the Middle East endured in the sixty years following the fall of the Ottoman Empire, you would be struck by the how small a role religion played in most of them. In only three short years during the Carter administration, this changed fundamentally, and the consequences are with us to this day.

First, in late 1978, the Islamic Revolution toppled the shah in Iran. The form of Shia Islam that Ayatollah Ruhullah Khomeini crafted in the hour of his victory was not remotely a return to tried-and-true religious practices, as he presented it. Like the greatest and most formidable revolutionaries throughout history, Khomeini proved to be a master at presenting radically new ways, usually the very opposite of the old ones he claimed to restore, in the camouflage of old, comforting images.

The Nazis championed the wholesome values of patriotism and family life while preparing genocidal wars of hitherto unimaginable horror. Likewise, Khomeini turned Shia Islam, for more than a millennium the most quiescent and politically passive form of Islam, into the prototype of a fierce new revolutionary fanaticism. He claimed the mantle of fundamentalism, but in reality was heavily influenced by the most murderous totalitarian secular ideologies of the century. This would not have been possible if a wise or competent president had been occupying the White House. President Jimmy Carter displayed consistent ignorance, complacency, and ineptitude in dealing with the mounting crisis in Iran. The end result was the worst humiliation the United States had ever experienced in the region and its expulsion from Iraq, less than a decade after President Richard Nixon had decided he would build it up as a major regional power and U.S. surrogate in the region.

The Islamic Revolution was really just the start of things to come. In November 1979, a year later, Iranian extremist students backed by Khomeini's revolutionary government stormed the U.S. embassy in Tehran and seized fifty-two Americans as hostages. They were held captive, abused, and in many cases tortured for 444 days.

Poisonous Prophet

Sayyid Qutb, one of the founders of modern radical Islam, studied in the United States and became convinced America was a den of depraved sexual iniquity. He didn't come to this conclusion after visiting Las Vegas, Manhattan, or Los Angeles, but after attending Protestant church socials in Greeley, Colorado, from 1948 to 1950. Qutb was also appalled by the American passion for sports, especially boxing, and for jazz, which he once described as "created by Negroes to satisfy their love of noise and to whet their sexual desires." He complained, too, that Americans were too restrictive about divorce (which in Islam is not a big deal). He remained a lifelong bachelor himself.

Qutb was the driving force of the Muslim Brotherhood in the early 1950s. More radical than Egyptian president Gamal Abdel Nasser—who wouldn't ban alcohol, and whom the Brotherhood tried to assassinate—Qutb and other Brotherhood leaders were arrested in 1954. Qutb spent a decade behind bars, where he wrote his book *Milestones*. In it he urged the universal application of *sharia* (Islamic law). He was executed in 1966, but his writings guided the radical revival of Sunni Islam in the late 1970s, and inspired Osama bin Laden.

Carter unerringly made the crisis worse. Instead of publicly downplaying it or distancing himself from it, while working privately to either threaten the Iranians or bring ruthless military force to bear on them, he grandiosely proclaimed his personal dedication to getting the hostages freed, wrongly imagining he could ride to reelection on a successful resolution of the affair. All he did was bog down the most powerful nation in the world in an apparently unending global humiliation.

Meanwhile, Khomeini's personal prestige and that of his revolution soared across the Middle East. Islamic fundamentalism, soon to hatch in the Sunni world as well, suddenly replaced the discredited model of Nasser's state socialism and alignment with Soviet Communism. The tough, ruthless, well-established dictatorships of Hafez Assad in Syria and Saddam Hussein in Iraq were not shaken or threatened. But they had no appeal beyond their own borders. Khomeini did.

In December 1979, Soviet president Leonid Brezhnev poured gasoline on the already burning fundamentalist flames, sending the Red Army into Afghanistan to put a Soviet favorite back into power. It proved to be the mother of all Soviet mess-ups.

For 160 years Afghanistan has been easy to conquer but impossible to hold. The British Empire conquered it three times between 1840 and 1920. The first time they made the mistake of trying to hold it. Literally less than a handful—fewer than five—of the 10,000 men made it back to India alive.

The Red Army suffered a very similar experience. They took Kabul within hours, and the tribes rose against them. It was widely seen as a jihad against godless atheists. The Soviets eventually lost 15,000 dead in a war that did much to discredit their regime and prepare the way for its fall. For President Reagan and his advisors, it seemed a heaven-sent opportunity to pay the Soviets back for bleeding the United States so badly in Vietnam. Just as Moscow had sent the North Vietnamese all the arms they needed, Reagan and his energetic director of Central Intelligence, William Casey, did the same thing for the mujahedin.

It was classic Reagan—acting shrewdly and subtly with a touch that Bismarck at his best could not equal. But in the long run there was a totally unanticipated and catastrophic "blowback" effect. Thousands of idealistic young Muslims from around the Middle East flocked to support the mujahedin. What the U.S. saw as a strike against our rival for global power, young Arab Muslims saw as a battle against godless infidel occupiers. The mujahedin became radicalized by the experience while getting an excellent grounding in modern guerrilla warfare. One of them came from one of the wealthiest, most prestigious families in Saudi Arabia. His name was Osama bin Laden.

Saudi Arabia, with the full approval of the United States, used its vast oil wealth to fund the mujahedin. Neither government dreamed of the true nature of the forces they were unleashing. Iran had successfully defied and humiliated one of the two thermonuclear superpowers in the hostage crisis and lived to tell the tale. Now the "muj" in Afghanistan were withstanding the Red Army, the most powerful military ground force on earth, an army that had not known defeat in war for more than sixty years.

The revolution drew blood in Egypt in 1981. President Nasser of Egypt, in 1966, had hanged Sayyid Qutb, the visionary prophet of the Sunni Ikhwan (Muslim Brotherhood), with impunity. Fifteen years after Qutb was hanged, soldiers in the Egyptian army broke ranks during a parade to celebrate the 1973 Yom Kippur War and gunned down Nasser's successor, Anwar Sadat. They were motivated by Qutb's fierce dreams.

Nasser's brutal state suppression of religion was the norm in the region. The blowback would have been contained to Sadat's assassination—and Qutb's ideas would not have caught fire—if not for the bungles of the Soviets in Afghanistan in 1979, and those of Jimmy Carter in undermining the shah and assuming that democracy would automatically succeed him.

(President George W. Bush, Defense Secretary Donald Rumsfeld, and their policymakers made exactly the same mistake about Iraq after Saddam a quarter century later.)

Dangerous new ideas were on the march.

Chapter 5

IRAN

Iran is a country many Americans think they know all about, but in reality they don't have the slightest clue. That is because our media and our textbooks give us a couple of clichés and then move on.

The Persian Empire: When Iran was good

The one thing any Christian or Jew raised on the Bible knows about Iran is that the Persian Empire, created 2,500 years ago under Cyrus and Darius the Great, was a good thing. It allowed the exiled Jews to return home from Babylon and rebuild their temple in Jerusalem.

In the seventh century, however, the Persian Empire collapsed, and the land that is now Iran became a Shiite Muslim domain—and it has remained thus for thirteen and a half centuries. Unlike Saudi Arabia, which did not exist until Abdulaziz ibn Saud crated it after World War I, Iran has been a coherent nation-state for more than five hundred years. Under the Safavid dynasty from 1501 to 1736, ruled by emperors known as shahs, Persia was one of the dozen or so empires that among them controlled nearly the entire human race. Under later dynasties after the Safavids, the Persians/Iranians were less formidable, but they maintained their independence proudly throughout. They were one of only a handful

Guess what?

- The deal Winston Churchill struck with the Iranians in 1913 remains a major factor in Iran's global oil strategy today.

- What happens when the U.S. meddles in Iran's politics? Ayatollah Khomeini and Mahmoud Ahmadinejad.

of nations in the Middle East and Asia to do so in the face of the global sweep of the great high-tech empires of the Western world.

Clash of empires: U.S. vs. Britain

Iran was a backwater through the nineteenth century. In 1908 its centuries of quietude ended with the discovery of significant reserves of oil. Within four years, the dynamic and visionary young Winston Churchill, then first lord of the admiralty, had set up the Anglo-Iranian Oil Company to secure and develop Iran's oil reserves as a reliable strategic fuel reserve for his navy, then still the strongest in the world. Anglo-Iranian Oil is still around today, having changed its name to British Petroleum (and now simply BP). And Churchill's bold move, done to secure the oil to power the turbine engines of Britain's revolutionary *Queen Elizabeth*–class battleships, became one of the handful of government initiatives that ever turned a fat profit for the taxpayer.

For the next forty years, the British taxpayer and Anglo-Iranian's shareholders made tremendous money from their Iranian operations. Iran

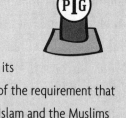

Ayatollah Khomeini's Thoughts on the White Revolution

"I have repeatedly pointed out that the government has evil intentions and is opposed to the ordinances of Islam....The Ministry of Justice has made clear its opposition to the ordinances of Islam by various measures like the abolition of the requirement that judges be Muslim and male; henceforth, Jews, Christians, and the enemies of Islam and the Muslims are to decide on affairs concerning the honor and person of the Muslims."

Ayatollah Ruhullah Khomeini, speech on March 22, 1963, in Qom, Iran

retained its political independence and the British pretty much ignored domestic developments as long as they could develop and extract the oil.

World War II bolstered Iran's importance because the country provided a safe and secure land bridge to ferry Lend/Lease supplies from Britain and America to the Soviet Union to help keep it in the war against Nazi Germany. When the shah at the time, Reza Shah, a peasant turned soldier turned general who had seized the throne in 1921, showed pro-Nazi sympathies, he was quickly and efficiently forced into exile. His son, Mohammad Reza Pahlavi, was established as a harmless figurehead. So peaceful was Iran that the Allies chose its capital, Tehran, for the first Big Three summit in 1943 between U.S. president Franklin Roosevelt, British prime minister Churchill, and Soviet dictator Josef Stalin.

Until the early 1950s, Iranians knew little about the United States and cared less, and Americans felt the same way about them. That changed during the fateful presidency of Dwight D. Eisenhower.

Mohammed Mosaddeq, a contemporary of Egyptian president Gamal Abdel Nasser—and like him a romantic, idealistic, left-wing, anti-Western demagogue—took power in Iran in 1951 and nationalized the British oil industry there. The British (Churchill, ironically, was prime minister again) were furious, but having just liquidated their Indian empire and been forced out of their Palestine Mandate, they were in no position to do anything about it.

Fearing an anti-American Iran, Eisenhower gave the CIA the green light to organize a military coup to topple Mosaddeq and give effective power back to Pahlavi, whom the British had installed back during World War II. It worked liked a charm.

But then the Western allies fell out. Iran's oil was worth big bucks, rivaling Iraq as the holder of the second-largest reserves of the stuff. The oil was also easily accessible and of high quality. Eisenhower made sure the U.S. oil majors got favored access to it. The British were forced out of the primary position they had enjoyed in Iran for more than forty years, and Churchill, who had made it all possible, was forced to swallow the deal.

The British were furious, but there was nothing they could do about it. From Washington's point of view it all seemed hunky-dory. But Eisenhower had planted the seeds for future destruction.

Liberal busybodies spark the Islamic Revolution

Eisenhower then pushed ahead and got the young shah to approve Iran's participation with Iraq, Turkey, and Pakistan in the Central Treaty Organization (CENTO), intended to be a Middle Eastern and South Asian extension of NATO (i.e., a tool for blocking the Soviet Union from expanding to the south into the Middle East and its oil fields).

Although Shah Pahlavi remained pro-Western (he had a taste for beautiful Western woman, Western nightlife, and parties on the Riviera), his people did not. The hatred and paranoia they had felt toward Britain for forty years was then shifted toward the United States for toppling Mosaddeq. That might not have mattered in the long term if the shah had left well enough alone and simply allowed free market economics and his bulging oil revenues to naturally raise living standards, or if he took care to respect his people's traditional ways, as the far wiser rulers of Saudi Arabia and Kuwait were doing across the Gulf. But he didn't.

For the shah had been infected by other Western passions. He was a liberal, social-reforming do-gooder. He imbibed the dominant political fashion of the time in Britain and America for socialism, big government, national planning, and social engineering. He called it his White Revolution. Millions of Iranians were uprooted from the land and forced into the towns and cities. While their standard of living rose, they missed their old, slow-moving, cherished way of life.

American liberals, especially in the media, loved it, and the shah was played up as a mixture of Winston Churchill, Franklin Roosevelt, and Mother Teresa. He was launching his own New Deal and curing the backward folk of their repressive traditions and religion. *Time* magazine was a particularly enthusiastic and witless booster. Only the Iranian people disagreed.

The shah's dependence on the United States and his honeymoon with Israel in the 1950s and 1960s deluded leaders in both countries that Iran was inherently moderate, anti-Arab, and pro-Western. They couldn't have been more wrong. Anti-American and anti-Israeli popular sentiment grew dramatically in Iran during those years.

At Least Something Good Came Out of It

The failure of the commando raid on Tehran to free the hostages resulted in the creation of U.S. Special Operations Command and the Army's 160th Special Operations Aviation Regiment: the "Night Stalkers."

Meanwhile, U.S. state-of-the-art aircraft, tanks, and automatic weapons flowed to the shah in an unending stream, with President Nixon's blessing. But within two years, the shah had turned upon and bitten the hand that fed him. He joined forces with Saudi Arabia, his nation's historic rival and enemy on the other side of the Gulf, and supported King Faisal in implementing an unprecedented quadrupling of the global price of oil in the winter of 1973–1974 through the Organization of the Petroleum Exporting Countries (OPEC). The U.S. domestic economy dropped as if pole-axed. Faisal and the shah overnight caused more damage to the United States than the Soviet Union, Communist China, and the Korean and Vietnam wars combined.

Amazingly, future presidents would mess up the Iran situation even more. In an eerie foreshadowing of disastrous U.S. policies of the early twenty-first century, Democratic president Jimmy Carter was so obsessed with fostering democracy and human rights in Iran that he fatally undermined and distracted the shah.

Like so many other big-government, reform-minded liberals before him, Pahlavi did not realize that by destroying the old traditions of society, he was also destroying the foundation his own regime rested on. The most conservative, backward (in the very best sense of the word), and peaceful society in the Middle East was transformed and modernized, pitched into restless motion. Iran was cut off from its own stable past, longing for it and yet ripe for radical change.

Enter Grand Ayatollah Ruhullah Khomeini, the Man in Black.

Ayatollah Khomeini: The fruit of American meddling

In 1977–1978, popular pressures on the shah and protests against him steadily grew. President Carter was insistent that the shah divest himself of much of his power and start to democratize Iran. At the very least, he had to rein in his own elite special forces and his secret police.

Meanwhile, Iran was transformed by a sudden wave of extreme Shiite Islamists, stirred up by the endless recorded sermons of an eminent but hitherto obscure cleric, one Ayatollah Ruhullah Khomeini, already in his late seventies and living in exile in Paris. Khomeini was backed by Iranian extreme leftists supported by motley sources ranging from the Soviet KGB to the Palestine Liberation Organization—all of them bitter enemies of the United States. Yet all Carter seemed to care about was lecturing the shah to improve his human rights record.

The U.S. government certainly didn't want the shah to fall, and if he did, senior U.S. policymakers hoped that a stable, democratic, pro-American coalition could be shepherded to power in his place. This fantasy was a striking contrast to what a more confident, competent CIA serving a vastly more competent president—Dwight Eisenhower—had managed to pull off in toppling the democratically elected Mohammed Mosaddeq to restore the shah to full power a quarter-century before. It was also remarkably similar to the fantasies that U.S. policymakers on the National Security Council and within the Pentagon harbored for their fantasy of a democratic and pro-American Iraq a quarter-century later.

Carter bumbled, micromanaged, ignored, pettifogged, and lectured the shah—and then he lost Iran. The shah fell and was forced to flee in January 1979. There was chaos on the streets. Khomeini came home to be greeted as the nation's greatest hero. A beaming Yasser Arafat flew in from southern Lebanon. Khomeini almost never smiled, but he was all grins and hugs for the Palestinian revolutionary leader. America's humiliation was only just beginning.

While all this was going on, incredibly, Carter delivered far more effort to brokering a final peace treaty between Israel and Egypt (which were already in a state of de facto peace, and both countries were already in the U.S. orbit).

Carter's standing in the opinion polls steadily declined. It didn't help that the dragon of inflation, briefly defeated by President Gerald Ford, was rising again. And in that same fateful year of 1979 the OPEC nations pushed through another massive oil price hike with newly radicalized Iran eagerly supporting it. As it had done six years before, the U.S. economy reeled.

Carter and the hostage crisis

On top of all that, Iranian "students" (they were actually revolutionary paramilitary forces acting with the full support of their government) stormed the U.S. embassy in Tehran and held fifty-two diplomats and

Ahmadinejad's Fighting Words

"If you would like to have good relations with the Iranian nation in the future, recognize the Iranian nation's right. Recognize the Iranian nation's greatness. And bow down before the greatness of the Iranian nation and surrender. If you don't accept, the Iranian nation will later force you to surrender and bow down."

Mahmoud Ahmadinejad, speech on August 15, 2006

other American citizens hostage. For 444 days these Americans were prisoners, regularly tortured and abused. Carter couldn't get them out. At one point, he approved a plan for U.S. Special Forces to launch a commando raid in the heart of Tehran to free them.

It was an exceptionally daring, dangerous, and risky concept to start with. U.S. troops were being sent into the heart of a capital city of eight million people, almost all of whom hated them. We had never tried this sort of thing before.

To make things even worse, Carter micromanaged again. At the last minute, he slashed the number of helicopters for the mission. For twenty years, the focus of U.S. military operations had been in the damp rain forests of Southeast Asia. American forces had done no serious desert fighting since the Italian and Nazi forces had surrendered to Eisenhower, Patton, and Bradley in Tunisia thirty-six years before. So the sand of the desert that jammed key helicopter mechanisms and caused one of them to crash came as a surprise. The mission was aborted. Details of it were soon discovered and revealed to the world. The U.S. national humiliation was complete.

To add to Carter's woes, and to underscore the complete contempt that Kremlin policymakers now had for him, in December 1979 Soviet president Leonid Brezhnev approved the invasion and effective takeover of Afghanistan. In less than nine months, the shining achievement of Camp David (as it seemed at the time) had been entirely overshadowed. The U.S. and Western position in the Middle East seemed to be crumbling by the hour.

Post-revolution Iran

The history of the Islamic Republic in the twenty-nine years since Ayatollah Khomeini seized power fits into four general periods:

1. The era of war and confrontation

2. The era of isolation

3. The era of (relative) moderation

4. The era of renewed belligerence

Khomeini was eager for war and confrontation. Like so many fanatical revolutionaries before him, from Robespierre in the French Revolution to Lenin in the Bolshevik Revolution, Khomeini was convinced that the perfection of his revolutionary ideas and teachings would sweep up millions of people in an irresistible tide. And like Robespierre and Lenin, he was wrong.

For Khomeini, Carter's folly was an ecstatic victory over the United States; nothing like it had been seen since Nasser's day nearly a quarter-century before. But the tide was about to change, thanks to America's secret weapon in the Middle East. His name was Saddam Hussein.

In September 1980, Saddam invaded Khuzestan, an oil-rich coastal province of Iran. He thought the Iranian revolutionary regime was tottering and that the Iranians would fall apart. It was the same mistake Adolf Hitler had made when he invaded the Soviet Union and set off a war to the death with Saddam's personal hero Josef Stalin.

What happened next should give any Americans and Israelis enthusiastic about invading Iran pause. The Iranian people rallied behind Khomeini, and as Iran's population was more than four times Iraq's, after a few months the tide turned and the Iraqis were forced back into their country.

Saddam sensibly sought peace, but Khomeini was implacable when aroused. He was determined to crush the Iraqi state and then sweep on across the Middle East. Heedless of the cost to his own people, he pushed forward. Teenage boys, including many as young as twelve, were recruited into fanatical suicide attack squads. Between half a million and a million Iranians were killed in the war, and possibly as many as 100,000 Iraqis died. As long as Khomeini lived, any armistice or compromise was out of the question and the suicide attacks and massacre of innocents continued. The Iraqis showed no hesitation in using poison gas—almost unknown in warfare since World War I—against the Iranians and killed perhaps 100,000 Iranian soldiers with it.

Finally, in 1988, even Khomeini was forced to recognize the inevitable and accept a compromise cease-fire. The act of peace-making probably proved too much for him; he died the following year at the ripe old age of eighty-six.

Moderation (relatively speaking) in Iran

For the next eight years, Iran remained very much in the international doghouse. Khomeini's nemesis, Saddam, emboldened by what he imag-

The Roots of Persian Belligerence?

"For these reasons, therefore, I am bent upon this war; and I see likewise therewith united no few advantages. Once let us subdue this people, and those neighbors of theirs...and we shall extend the Persian territory as far as God's heaven reaches. The sun will then shine on no land beyond our borders; for I will pass through Europe from one end to the other, and with your aid make of all the lands which it contains one country. For thus, if what I hear be true, affairs stand: the nations whereof I have spoken, once swept away, there is no city, no country left in all the world, which will venture so much as to withstand us in arms. By this course then we shall bring all mankind under our yoke, alike those who are guilty and those who are innocent of doing us wrong."

Persian king Xerxes, rallying his people to invade Athens and Sparta, as reported by Herodotus in *The Histories*

ined was success—though it had cost his country scores of billions of dollars and at least 100,000 lives—followed the war by invading Kuwait only two years later and bringing the wrath of the United States on his head.

Saddam's humiliation and the virtual destruction of his great army, the fourth largest in the world at the time, in the 1991 Gulf War was welcome news to the ayatollahs ruling in Tehran. But now the United States was stronger in the region than ever, especially following the collapse of the Soviet Union at the end of 1991. The Iranians remained isolated until 1997, when a relative moderate, President Mohammad Khatami, was elected as president of the Islamic Republic.

Khatami's two terms of leadership from 1997 to 2005 marked the third era of the history of the Islamic Republic. The United States remained the invincible superpower, and Saddam, though humbled, continued to rule in Baghdad amid many media reports of his renewed programs to develop powerful weapons of mass destruction. Iranians—both in the leadership and general population—were still terrified of the ogre who had inflicted so much suffering on them, so Iranian leaders continued to tread carefully between Baghdad and Washington. They gingerly improved their diplomatic and trade ties with the nations of Asia and Western Europe. China and India both had growing demands for their oil. And Khatami even sought to mend his country's long-destroyed ties with the United States. He offered to both the Clinton and Bush administrations to scrap Iran's nuclear program in return for a guarantee that the United States would recognize the Islamic Republic and respect its sovereignty.

With the benefit of hindsight, the deal could have worked. It would have been subject to verification. President George W. Bush would eventually agree to a far more limited and problematic agreement with North Korea on restricting its nuclear development.

Such a deal would have been of crucial benefit to Israel. In the first decade of the twenty-first century, it became clear that the Iranian nuclear program posed probably the gravest threat to the existence of the Jewish state since its creation. But ironically, pro-Israel activists in Washington were the loudest in urging its rejection. Khatami had humbled his country and begged for peace, but was sent away from the table.

Democracy's bitter gift: Mahmoud Ahmadinejad

Unable to deliver improved ties with the United States, Iranian voters took a new direction in 2005, electing a president fond of a mock turtleneck and blazer. Mahmoud Ahmadinejad brought in the fourth era of the Islamic Republic: renewed belligerence and confrontation with the United States and Israel.

During Khatami's eight years as president of Iran, the usual babbling pundits and armchair strategists in the United States endlessly asserted that it did not matter who was chief executive of Iran and that all Iranian leaders were really identical hard-line arch-villains who should never be mollified.

But when Ahmadinejad replaced Khatami, it soon became clear that who the leader was mattered a great deal. Ahmadinejad was open in his determination to develop nuclear weapons and ready to defy the whole world if necessary. He sought to delegitimize Israel's existence and boasted about obliterating it in language not heard since the heydays of Nasser and Saddam. He purged the Iranian government of relative moderates and put his hard-line allies into every key national security and military post he could. He also made no secret of his passionate loyalty to the vanished Twelfth Imam of Shiite Islam, and even ordered minutes of every Iranian cabinet meeting to be dropped down the well where the Twelfth Imam was said to have vanished.

Ahmadinejad was able to get away with this outrageous behavior because one enormous miscalculation had reversed twenty-four years of continual military defeat, massive casualties, diplomatic isolation, and strategic fear: the United States had invaded Iraq and toppled Saddam Hussein in 2003. By doing so, the Bush administration removed both enemies the ayatollahs most feared at a single stroke—Saddam and the United States itself.

For in the years following the toppling of Saddam, the 130,000 to 160,000 U.S. troops in Iraq were tied down, suffering slow but steady casualties from Sunni Muslim insurgents. Following the implementation of new strategies by General David Petraeus in 2007, which sought to cooperate with existing local Sunni leaderships in Anbar Province, the Sunni insurgency at last began to run out of steam. But by then, all of southern Iraq was run by local Shiite militias sympathetic to and backed by Iran, and the Shiite-dominated government of Prime Minister Nouri al-Maliki in Baghdad was seeking warm ties with Tehran as well.

Far from being a threat to Iran by being based in a strong ally next door, the U.S. ground forces in Iraq, with their communications lines to Kuwait and the Gulf running through Shiite militia–controlled territory, were increasingly at the mercy of Shiite groups sympathetic to Iran. No wonder Ahmadinejad was so bold and confident.

The U.S. invasion and occupation of Iraq therefore reversed a highly successful process of attrition, exhaustion, and containment that had handicapped the Islamic Revolution in Iran for the previous twenty-four years. Neo-Wilsonian liberal nation-building had failed yet again.

Iran on borrowed time

But by 2008 there was another factor driving the Iranians to more hardline policies: the Islamic Republic was running out of oil—and therefore out of time.

Iran's oil fields had been developed earlier and more vigorously than those of any Gulf nation. They were energetically pumping oil for the Anglo-Iranian Oil Company and Britain's Royal Navy for twenty years before Ibn Saud even signed his epochal agreement with Standard Oil of California to authorize the prospecting that led to the discovery of Saudi Arabia's great Dhahran oil fields. By the early years of the twenty-first century, the Iranians were already importing natural gas to pump pressure into their depleted fields. Far from threatening to become a swing producer, it was clear that after a few more years of peak production, Iran would be lucky to be a dangling producer, holding onto its market share in OPEC by the skin of its teeth.

If Iran's oil reserves had been discovered and developed in the 1930s, like Saudi Arabia's, then today the Islamic Republic would still be sitting pretty, enjoying enormous financial and mineral resources for decades to come, but Winston Churchill's energy and vision in getting the oil pumping by World War I meant that by 2008 the ayatollahs were living on borrowed time. That meant they had to push for maximum global prices in the OPEC cartel to get the maximum profits they could from their remaining oil. And it meant they had a far more pressing motive to try to seize the still enormous oil reserves of Iraq and Saudi Arabia for themselves by exporting the Islamic Revolution to them if they got the chance. Nearly a century after he made the deal, Churchill's epochal Anglo-Iranian oil venture was still driving destiny in the Middle East.

Chapter 6

THE ISRAELI-ARAB WARS
1947–1973

For the first quarter-century of its existence, the State of Israel was locked in a continual struggle for survival against its hostile Arab neighbors. In twenty-five years, Israel fought five major wars—and won all of them. How did the Israelis do it?

Israel, we're often told, is either a puppet state—or the puppet master—of the United States, and demolished its Arab neighbors on the strength of an American-created military superiority.

You used to hear this only from Arabs, but the myth has now seeped into the writings of anti-Zionist Jewish intellectuals and American left-wing polemicists. Any evidence—and there is a *lot* of it—that disproves their thesis is suppressed or simply ignored. The Israelis won their wars because they *had* to—and their military thinking and execution was of the highest caliber.

Death almost at birth

Israel's first war was by far the worst. When the Israelis drove the British out in 1947, they foolishly thought their troubles were over. They were now an independent country. But the British had been their protectors as well as occupiers of Palestine. Happy to be rid of their troublesome United Nations mandate in Palestine, the British were confident that the

Guess what?

- Israel's greatest general learned key tactical lessons from the Bible and from Germany's best panzer general

- France, not the United States, was Israel's best friend for the first twenty years of its existence.

- Golda Meir was a bungling politician who nearly destroyed her own country in the 1973 Yom Kippur War.

Arab Legion of Transjordan—a force led, equipped, trained, and officered by the British—would destroy the Jewish state at birth. They also assumed that the remaining Jews would become *dhimmis*: a tolerated minority inferior in political, human, and religious rights to the Muslim majority. Field Marshal Bernard Montgomery, the greatest British World War II general, was chief of the Imperial General Staff at the time, and this was his view.

It didn't work out that way. The Arabs launched a multi-pronged attack on Israel. Most important, perhaps, was when the Arab Legion crossed the Jordan River. It was welcomed by rapturous crowds in the hill regions north and south of Jerusalem (now known as the West Bank). In Jerusalem, it was a different story. The Legion couldn't make a direct move against the organized Jewish majority in West Jerusalem, but did receive support from the Arab majority into the ancient Old City, which is surrounded by a formidable, Turkish-built wall nearly four hundred years old. The Jewish Quarter of the Old City was besieged, and the Jewish paramilitary groups in West Jerusalem couldn't break through to relieve them.

Elsewhere, the main threat to the Israelis came from Palestinian Arab irregulars led by Abd al-Qadir al-Husseini, nephew of Haj Amin al-Husseini, the pro-Nazi mufti of the Palestinian Muslims. Like all great military leaders, Abd al-Qadir knew the strengths and weaknesses of the peasant irregulars he led. He knew that while brave, ferocious, and determined to fight for their homeland, they lacked military discipline and could not be organized to carry out ambitious, complex military operations. He knew that

A Book You're Not Supposed to Read

Thomas Kiernan was no lover of Israel or the Zionists, which makes his biography *Arafat: The Man and the Myth* (New York: W. W. Norton, 1976) all the more devastating. Alone among Arafat's many (and usually fawning) biographers, Kiernan questioned the official versions skeptically and dug deep, interviewing many people who had known Arafat as a boy.

they also lacked the heavier weapons that Israeli forces had, thanks to the foresight of Israel's David Ben-Gurion, who had stockpiled such weapons knowing that such a war was inevitable. Abd al-Qadir realized that his peasant irregulars were at their best in cutting off the land communications that were the Jews' most vulnerable point.

The winding, twisting, scenic road up to Jerusalem soon became the strategic axis of the war. The Palestinians cut off the 100,000 Jews in Jerusalem from Tel Aviv and farm settlements around the country, severing the supply line. The infant Jewish provisional government in Tel Aviv hastily organized makeshift armored convoys (riveting armor plates on trucks) to resupply Jerusalem.

But casualties were high. In a remarkable March 1994 speech given in Washington to the American Israel Public Affairs Committee, then Israeli prime minister Yitzhak Rabin vividly described the screams of his dying young Palmach friends—male and female soldiers burnt alive in the trucks that had been ambushed while crawling up to Jerusalem.

The tide turns

Eventually, Jewish commanders, including Yitzhak Rabin, denuded other fronts to bring a formidable force to clear the hills on either side of the road to Jerusalem. The fighting was ferocious. The key heights above Castel changed hands several times. But discipline and motivation were much higher among the Israeli soldiers than the Palestinian Arab ones. Many of the Arabs went home to their families without telling senior officers. An increasingly desperate Abd al-Qadir was killed at the front. His death was a devastating blow to the Palestinians, who have never had another leader to match him for military skill and charisma.

Meanwhile, Jewish settlements held off large numbers of Arab military forces, both conventional and irregular. Surprisingly, the Arab armies drafted from the Fertile Crescent and operating from Syria had a negligible impact on the war. In fact, the performance of the Iraqi, Syrian, and Egyptian armies, all of them conscripted peasant forces that had been miserably trained, equipped, and led, was very disappointing. Only the professional Arab Legion of Transjordan acquitted itself well. Not only did the Legion conquer and hold the West Bank (a walk-over) and Jerusalem (a considerable achievement in terms of the fierce fighting there), but it also held the key fortress of Latrun, a monastery looking out over rolling wheat fields in the Judean hills. The Israeli forces fought and lost three battles trying to take Latrun. David Ben-Gurion and his far too influential American advisor, Mickey Marcus, were obsessed with it. Hundreds of young Israeli soldiers died there for no strategic purpose.

By the end of the war, large supplies of weapons primarily from an arms deal with Czechoslovakia were giving the Israeli forces superior firepower and mobility at long last. Yigael Allon, the outstanding Israeli combat general of the war, swept into the Negev and secured Israel's claim to it. He outmaneuvered and trapped a large Egyptian force and was in a position to conquer the Sinai Peninsula as well. The Arab states sued for an armistice, and a lasting one was finally concluded on the Greek island of Rhodes in 1949.

The war ended in victory for the new state of Israel, but the cost was enormously high. Of the population of the infant state—600,000 including men, women, and children—some 6,000 died in the war, a full 1 percent. In the twenty-first-century United States, that would be the equivalent of a war in which three million people died.

Who's a Palestinian?

If you asked anyone in Palestine—Arab or Jew—from 1920 to 1947, "Who are the Palestinians?" the answer would be unequivocal: Palestinians were Jews, not Arabs. The quickly growing Jewish community in Palestine during this time always described itself as *Palestinian*. This usage

Hizzoner the Mayor Who Saved Jerusalem

Full-scale religious wars haven't broken out in the city of Jerusalem over the last forty years, and most of the credit should go to one man: Teddy Kollek, the Mayor Giuliani of Jerusalem. He became mayor in 1965, after an already distinguished political career. Before the 1967 war that united the city, it was divided like Berlin. Sometimes Jordanian soldiers used women and children in the poor Israeli neighborhoods (made up of Sephardic Jews exiled from Arab countries) for target practice—and they shot to kill. The Jordanians forbade Israeli Jews from crossing into the Old City or visiting Jewish graves on the Mount of Olives. Some Arabs used the ancient gravestones as toilet seats.

But the Six-Day War transformed the city, reuniting it on Israeli terms. Kollek revived Jerusalem with everything from world-class concert halls, theaters, parks, and even municipal latrines. He was the greatest builder in Jerusalem's history since King Solomon and Herod the Great. Unlike them, he wasn't a tyrant or an egomaniac, but merely wanted a beautiful, peaceful city, modeled a bit on his native and beloved Vienna, to the point of covering Jerusalem with flower displays. He also was determined to prove that Israel would be an open and fair custodian of Christian and Muslim holy places. Like the old Austrian empire from which he sprang, he honored the idea of the mosaic and could be seen at every celebration or festival of the city's myriad religious and ethnic communities. He obsessed over the tiniest details of his metropolis. Kollek was tough on law and order, enforced cleanliness, and maintained a high level of public services, delighting in making surprise inspections at hospitals and schools to keep the bureaucrats on their toes.

Jerusalem was, in general, an astonishing haven of peace for thirty-three years, until the second Palestinian intifada began in fall 2000, seven years after Kollek had left the mayor's office. One can't help but think that Jerusalem's Palestinian Arabs didn't appreciate how good they had it.

was still recognized in 1960 when the hit movie *Exodus* was made. Palestinian Arabs invariably referred to themselves as *Arabs*.

The war of 1947–1948 to eliminate the Jewish state at birth was fought by the Palestinian Arab community not as *Palestinians* but as *Arabs*. A distinct Palestinian Arab identity certainly emerged as a reaction to the massive Jewish immigration into Palestine, but it was not a millennia-old attachment to the country or the name.

Palestinian identity changed dramatically during the 1950s. The Palestinian Jews who had called themselves *Palestinians* for nearly thirty years now dropped that label and called themselves *Israelis* instead. Meanwhile, the hundreds of thousands of Palestinian refugees displaced by the war were bottled up in miserable refugee camps, primarily in Egypt-controlled Gaza, the West Bank, and to a lesser degree in southern Lebanon. The governments of Egypt, Jordan, and Lebanon did not want to risk destabilizing their societies by giving the refugees full citizenship, and so these Arabs had no home but the refugee camps—which, interest-

Arafat the Murderer

When U.S. president Bill Clinton embraced PLO chairman Yasser Arafat on the White House lawn in September 1993 when the Oslo Peace Accords were signed, did he know, or care, that Arafat had personally ordered the execution of U.S. ambassador Cleo Noel in 1973?

We know this because the CIA, which hadn't yet been gutted by Jimmy Carter, was tapping Arafat's phone and recorded him giving the order. President Richard Nixon's reaction was to vastly increase cooperation between the CIA and the Israeli Mossad to fight Palestinian terrorism.

ingly, provided excellent education for the youth. The well-funded United Nations Relief and Works Agency maintained the best possible basic standards of health care in those camps. Conditions were actually better than endured by the rural peasantry in Syria and Egypt until the 1950s and after. And within a decade the Palestinian Arabs became the best-educated ethnic group in the Arab world. If the United Nations of the 1950s was the benign hand of postwar Western imperialism, the Palestinian Arabs benefited greatly from its emphasis on improving education and health care.

By the mid to late 1960s, wealthy nations like Saudi Arabia and the Gulf oil states were importing tens of thousands of Palestinians for skilled labor, such as teaching, plumbing, electrical maintenance, and engineering. The Palestinian Arabs became the "can-do" upper working class and professional middle class of the Arab world. But still, the vast majority of them continued to fester in the camps.

The older generations of Palestinian Arabs who had fought the Zionist enterprise and growing Jewish settlement so long throughout the British Mandate period had been overwhelmingly rural peasants. Even while the overall standard of living in Palestine and opportunities for more prosperous lives in towns and cities grew during British rule, the fiercest centers of opposition to the Jewish settlement erupted in reaction to legal Zionist Jewish organizations purchasing usually extremely low-grade land, like the swamps of the Jezreel Valley or on the coast, as the main centers for building kibbutzim (collective farms) and other settlements. Thus Arab opposition stemmed from the peasantry, and took the form of relatively random attacks against Jewish civilians traveling alone or caught at vulnerable moments.

This pattern continued, though in much intensified form, in the first generation of guerrilla attacks during the 1950s. At first, the infant Israeli army proved ineffectual at deterring or responding to these attacks, and was unable to knock out the bases they came from. During his crucial years as the Israeli army chief of staff (1953 to 1957), Lieutenant General Moshe Dayan reshaped the military to combat such attacks. In 1956, in coordination with the Anglo-French move against Egypt's illegal nationalization of the Suez Canal, Israel seized the Gaza Strip and Sinai in response to cross-border terrorism and Egypt's closing of the Suez Canal to Israeli shipping. After that campaign and the demilitarization of the Sinai Peninsula, guerrilla attacks were dramatically reduced and the Palestinian Arab guerrilla movement appeared to be over.

That changed in 1964 when a young Palestinian Arab related to Hitler's old ally, Haj Amin al-Husseini, created the Fatah organization. He would later make it the dominant faction of the Palestine Liberation Organization. His name was Yasser Arafat. Arafat's first tactical victory in 1964 was a purely verbal one, but inspired. He appropriated the name *Palestinian*—which had been used exclusively by Palestinian Jews—for the Palestinian Arab people. It has been exclusively applied and used in this way ever since.

Adopting the term *Palestinian* sharpened and legitimized the nature of the Palestinian Arab opposition to the very existence of the State of Israel. It also served to shroud the essential underlying religious and existential nature of the conflict. It was certainly true that the Palestinian Arab people from the very beginning overwhelmingly opposed the Jewish return to the ancestral land of both peoples.

The 1948 invasion of Palestine by the Arab armies was represented to the West as a campaign to rescue Palestinian Arabs from Jewish oppressors. In Arab countries it was presented unambiguously as a war to destroy the Zionist state. In the West, Arafat downplayed the underlying religious and potentially genocidal aspects of his anti-Zionist campaign. If the Palestinian Arabs were the Palestinian people, then they were obviously eligible for national rights of "self-determination." As various Western-built empires crumbled, the United Nations and the

United States both professed to support national "self-determination" around the globe.

Redefining the Arab-Israeli struggle as a national conflict between two different nationalisms changed the debate from Muslims vs. Jews. It became diplomatically respectable. It put the PLO and Fatah firmly in the camp of countless other national liberation movements supported by leftists in the liberal democratic West. It also had the considerable advantage of being true as far as it went.

There had been no Palestinian Arab nationalism during the long centuries of the Ottoman Empire. But the conditions of living under British rule after World War I, while a new Jewish national society was being built up at breakneck speed around them, had certainly given the Palestinian Arabs a very different experience from that of peoples in any other part of the Arab world. And the experience of the hundreds of thousands who fled their homes or were expelled by Israeli forces in the 1948 war into the miserable refugee camps, with their bizarre but significant combination of excellent basic health care, superb education, and otherwise awful conditions, made that national experience more distinctive still. If the Palestinian Arab people were not a cohesive national group in 1948, they certainly were twenty years later.

The real Yasser Arafat

Yasser Arafat dominated the Palestinian national movement for forty years, with dire results for his own people. In many important respects, he was not at all what he appeared to be.

Arafat claimed to have been born in Jerusalem, but was actually born in Egypt and grew up in Gaza. He presented the PLO as a fashionably Marxist-socialist revolutionary movement—a stance that won him a quarter-century of loyal support from the Kremlin. But there is convincing evidence that he started his underground career, and made his first power base in revolutionary Arab politics, with the Ikhwan, the Muslim Brotherhood in Gaza and Egypt.

He presented to the world an image of being an incorruptible, selfless revolutionary, but he stashed away billions of dollars during his long domination of the Palestinian national movement, and his Fatah was always mired in corruption and incompetence.

Arafat presented to the world the face of an Arab region unified in its opposition to Israel, but he killed many Arabs during his long career. In his heyday, every Arab country that gave refuge to him and the PLO was ruined and plunged into civil war as a result. King Hussein of Jordan drove the PLO out of his country in September 1970. Lebanon then took them in. They established a powerful enclave in southern Lebanon known as "Fatahland." But unlike the much more formidable Hezbollah, which eventually succeeded them, they proved militarily useless against Israel except for a handful of raids that slaughtered Israeli civilians, including more than twenty children in at school in Ma'alot in 1974. Starting in 1975, the PLO plunged Lebanon into fifteen years of civil war and anarchic violence that eventually took 150,000 lives.

Many Arab leaders hated Arafat or distrusted him ferociously—notably King Hussein of Jordan, President Anwar Sadat of Egypt, and most of all, President Hafez Assad of Syria.

Arafat was a very poor organizer and administrator but an extremely shrewd political tactician and utterly ruthless gang leader and revolutionary. He was a master of the shakedown. The Saudis and Gulf Arab leaders paid Arafat protection money, knowing that if they didn't, the PLO's assassins and political subversives would be sicced on them. European leaders during and after the Oslo Peace Process gave even more, but for all their talk, they never raised a finger to make sure the money was being spent properly. (In fact, it was being siphoned off into Swiss bank accounts and used to create the terror arsenal that later killed more than a thousand Israeli civilians during the Second Intifada.) The Clinton administration and its acclaimed peace diplomats were totally asleep at the switch as well.

Arafat was almost a diplomat of genius, but he regularly overplayed his hand. He won pan-Arab and global recognition for his national movement, only to provoke ferocious Israeli retaliation. He refused to compromise until he was forced to, which doomed him and the movement he led to almost three decades of endless military and ultimately political defeats. After that, however, the Oslo Peace Process finally gave him political power, which he squandered over the next decade, leaving Fatah and the PLO exhausted, discredited, and bankrupt in the face of a new, far more implacable, and formidable religious revolutionary organization: Hamas, the Islamic Resistance Movement. However, throughout his

What Did Romanian Intelligence Know about Arafat?

Lieutenant General Ion Mihai Pacepa, the former head of the Romanian intelligence service, writes often about Arafat in his startling book, *Red Horizons*. He mentions how the Communist-era Romanian government spied on Arafat and taped him cavorting in a homosexual dalliance with his bodyguard. The Romanians also compiled an unexpurgated file on Arafat, which documented a litany "of tangled oriental political maneuvers, of lies, of embezzled PLO funds deposited in Swiss banks, and of homosexual relationships, beginning with his teacher and ending with his current bodyguards. After reading that report, I felt a compulsion to take a shower whenever I had been kissed by Arafat, or even just shaken his hand."

career, Arafat could always count on his political charm and guile to carry him and the PLO from one defeat and exile into another.

Arafat, Fatah, and the PLO did not hold national democratic elections in the camps (or anywhere else) to confirm themselves as the named national representatives of the Palestinian people, in 1964 or in the years that followed. They couldn't. The Palestinian refugee camps remained under foreign control: Egyptian and Jordanian until 1967, and Israeli thereafter.

Arafat and his Fatah were by no means the only group claiming the mantle of revolutionary representatives of the Palestinian people. The Popular Front for the Liberation of Palestine, the Palestine Liberation Army, and other smaller groups soon sprang up. Iraq and Syria both either set up or gave shelter and limited support to different groups.

Egypt's fight to destroy Israel

Gamal Abdel Nasser took Egypt's reins of power publicly in 1954 and quickly accrued one triumph after another. He boldly nationalized the Suez Canal and defied the Anglo-French military reoccupation of the Canal Zone in 1956. Within a few weeks, Soviet and American pressure forced the British and French to leave the canal and forced the Israelis to pull out of Sinai. This diplomatic "victory" erased, in the eyes of the Egyptian people, Egypt's obvious military defeat and solidified Nasser's status as a hero. Nasser stood in striking contrast to the leader he had deposed: the fat, corrupt, and selfish King Farouq. Nasser inaugurated ambitious social policies to bring education and basic health care to the Egyptian people, socialized the economy, and treated political critics with relative leniency, compared to later regional tyrants like Hafez Assad and Saddam Hussein.

Still, Nasser was a Soviet-style socialist and proud of it. While wrecking his country's economy, he sought to conquer his neighbors. He pursued the megalomaniacal policy of destabilizing and then toppling the remaining pro-Western, moderate monarchies of the Arab world, especially those in Iraq, Libya, Saudi Arabia, and Jordan.

At first, all seemed to go in his favor. The royal family of Iraq was slaughtered in the horrific military coup of 1958. An alarmed Syria agreed to form a United Arab Republic under Nasser's leadership. King Hussein's days on this earth appeared numbered as Nasser's agents and sympathizers unleashed one assassination plot after another against him. (He survived more than twenty-five of them.) And an eager Soviet Union bet all its Middle East chips on Nasser, concluding enormous arms deals with him. On the eve of the 1967 Six-Day War, even Field Marshal Bernard Montgomery, the desert conqueror of Erwin Rommel in World War II, concluded after a visit to Egypt that the Israeli army would have no chance against Egypt's new legions.

Nasser sent Egyptian troops to establish and support a puppet regime in remote Yemen, at the opposite end of the Red Sea, while his agents maintained a campaign of terrorism in the British-controlled Protectorate of Aden that eventually succeeded in driving the British out.

Backed by his mighty Soviet ally, Nasser looked well on the way to conquering the entire Middle East. The weak, short-sighted British governments of Harold Wilson and Edward Heath, who were determined only to pull out of the region, offered little opposition. The United States, meanwhile, was caught up in the Vietnam War and domestic upheaval. It seemed that no one would or could stop Nasser. Even the Saudis trembled.

In 1967, however, Nasser pushed Israel too far, and all his pretensions were spectacularly and cruelly exposed. The Egyptians demanded, successfully, that United Nations peacekeeping troops be withdrawn from Sinai—a clear provocation and prelude to war. Nasser moved 1,000 tanks and 100,000 Egyptian soldiers to threaten Israel, and in a semi-replay of the Suez crisis of 1956, closed the Straits of Tiran to Israeli ships. He also knew that Syria (which was periodically shelling northern Israel) and Jordan (which harbored the PLO), both of which had signed defense treaties with him, were ready to attack the Jewish state.

Nasser wasn't just grandstanding or scrapping for some turf. His aim was to wipe out Israel. His quasi-genocidal aims against Israel should not be doubted. His speeches and the overall rhetoric of his regime were unrelenting in their determination to annihilate the Jewish state. His military buildup, supplied by the Soviets, was focused entirely on Israel from the very beginning. Most of all, Nasser's darkest and most ambitious military program had literally genocidal ambitions. He employed as many German former Nazi scientists as he could on twin programs to develop ballistic missiles capable of reaching Israel and biological warheads for them.

The Israeli secret service, the Mossad, managed to kill a couple of the scientists involved in Nasser's biological warfare plan, scaring off the rest. A key Israeli intelligence officer in directing this crucial operation was Yitzhak Shamir, the former head of the Freedom Fighters for Israel, or Lehi, in the 1945–1947 guerrilla war against the British.

There was no reason why Nasser could not have carried out a cautious accommodation with Israel, at the very least, through the 1950s and 1960s. For most of that time, King Hussein of Jordan, from a vastly weaker position, had succeeded in doing just that.

Egypt's huge and rapidly growing population and its massive poverty should have been Nasser's main area of concern. Had he opened Egypt's borders with the Palestinian refugee camps in Gaza, he would have helped the plight of these Arab refugees and enriched his country with excellent young Palestinian professionals then starting to be trained in the well-funded, well-run refugee camp schools. If he had truly been looking after his people's welfare, Nasser would have welcomed from those camps the doctors, teachers, plumbers, auto mechanics, construction engineers, and electricians Egypt so desperately needed.

Instead, Nasser opted for arrogance, ambition, and wars of conquest and extermination. He doomed his people to a cycle of three more wars, the devastation of many of the nation's largest and previously most prosperous cities, and the worst military humiliations in their modern history.

The Soviet Union vs. Israel

In the Six-Day War, the Israelis knew they couldn't wait to be attacked. They struck first, destroying nearly three-quarters of the Egyptian air force, routing the Egyptian army of Sinai, repelling the Jordanian attack and capturing the West Bank, and hurling back the Syrians and taking the Golan Heights.

All this is well known. What is less well known is that the Soviet Union considered attacking Israel itself. The Soviets had warned Nasser that the Israelis might launch a preemptive strike, but the Soviet role went far beyond supplying arms and intelligence to the Arabs. A book published in 2007, *Foxbats over Dimona*, documented how Soviet MiG-25 fighters had flown reconnaissance missions over the Israeli nuclear plant at Dimona. The Soviets knew the Israelis were developing nuclear weapons and wanted to stop them. The Soviets were even preparing for a major amphibious landing and preemptive strikes of their own to destroy the Dimona reactor. In the end, the Israelis won the war so quickly the Soviets never got a chance to jump in.

Like his Soviet masters, Nasser was not fearful of the Israeli army and gravely underestimated it. He and his top commanders also completely underestimated

Books You're Not Supposed to Read

Six Days of War: June 1967 and the Making of the Modern Middle East by Michael B. Oren; New York: Presidio Press, 2003.

Now forgotten in America but very revealing about the professional excellence the Israelis worked so hard to create in their army in the 1960s is *The Tanks of Tammuz* by Shabtai Teveth; New York: Viking, 1969.

Israel's air strike capability. They especially had no conception of how the Israelis could multiply their air striking power by rapidly refueling and rearming their planes and sending them out for second and third strikes on the same day. Nasser's blood-curdling threats of exterminating Israel turned into stark Arab humiliation.

Was Israel really in danger in 1967?

It has become fashionable among Israeli leftists and liberals in recent decades to acclaim Israel's then prime minister Levi Eshkol as a wise statesman, restrained and moderate in peace and brilliantly successful in war. The truth was, as the Israeli public well recognized at the time, Eshkol was a corrupt old apparatchik who had put Israel into a economic recession, spiritual depression, and suffering from more emigrants than immigrants. He also folded under pressure. When the Egyptian army flooded into Sinai, Eshkol addressed the nation. It was a disaster. He trembled and stuttered and looked like what he was—a burned out, ineffectual, and very frightened little old man.

At that moment, the most important figure in keeping the Israel Defense Forces running and on alert was the chief of operations and former air force commander, General Ezer Weizman, the nephew of the nation's first president, Chaim Weizmann. (Ezer spelled his name with one *n* instead of two to indicate his disapproval of his uncle, whom he regarded as too dovish and ready to rely on the British). He knew that unless he acted, Israel could expect tens of thousands dead from Egyptian air attacks and ground assault. In desperation, Eshkol conceded the need to create a new national unity government. Longtime chief opposition leader Menachem Begin of the Herut Party, whom the ruling socialists regarded as a useless, melodramatic blowhard, was brought in as a minister without portfolio and proved to be a hawkish but constructive and stabilizing presence. But the key appointment went to Moshe Dayan. Just as Neville Chamberlain in 1939 was forced to bring back Winston

Churchill as political head of Britain's Royal Navy, Eshkol was forced to hand over his military portfolios and appoint Dayan minister of defense.

Dayan's impact was immediate and electrifying. He transformed national morale and provided a decisive, activist, political-strategic direction to the nation that Eshkol, Abba Eban, Golda Meir, and Rabin had utterly failed to provide.

He gave a press conference stating—correctly—the real strength of the Israeli armed forces. He indicated that the crisis was likely to be peacefully resolved and thereby lulled the Egyptians and their allies into assuming that Israel would continue to act as passively as it had under Eshkol and his colleagues. He also won the everlasting gratitude of U.S. president Lyndon Johnson for making quite clear that Israel would not need the U.S. armed forces to protect it. (Dayan had visited Vietnam and correctly assessed how America's political and military leadership were bungling the war.) The American public breathed a sigh of relief that American troops would not be needed in the Middle Eastern crisis. They breathed an even bigger one a week later when Dayan unleashed the Israeli air force on the Egyptians and smashed forever Nasser's dark dreams.

The miraculous victory

The Israeli military victory in the Six-Day War was even more sudden and overwhelming than the brilliant U.S. victory in the first Gulf War—and was done without all the time for preparation that America and its allies had. The Israeli victory was a tribute to the reserve system that General Yigael Yadin had designed almost two decades before, and it was executed with a brilliance seldom seen in the chaos of war. Responding to defeat, Nasser propagated the big lie: Israeli military success was yet another British and American plot. He may even have believed it. Because Egyptian aircraft couldn't fly multiple sorties per day, the Egyptians never dreamed the Israelis could. They therefore assumed that the waves of planes that had wiped out their air force and their allies' air forces could not possibly all have come from Israel. The U.S. Sixth Fleet in the Mediterranean must have provided its aircraft carriers and planes, and probably the British had too. Wild anti-American rioting immediately broke out all over the Arab world, which is a ready market for conspiracy theories to cover up Arab ignominy, failure, and defeat.

Nasser was dishonest even with his Arab allies. He called King Hussein of Jordan and told him the Israelis had lost the first day of air fighting and therefore were now doomed to be destroyed. He urged Hussein to enter the war immediately. The king, ironically, owed his survival to Israel for staring down Syria in 1958, when the Syrians had threatened to invade Jordan. He also owed his own intelligence service, which had protected him from numerous Nasser-masterminded assassination attempts. But King Hussein also knew his public hated Israel and he could be toppled by popular rage if he stayed out of the war. So he temporized by allowing his military forces in and around Jerusalem to bombard the Jewish half of the city.

The bombardment was relatively light, and because Israel's civilian shelter measures in Jerusalem were good, casualties were negligible. But for a country that had appeared to be surrounded by implacable enemies and on the brink of being extinguished by them, it proved to be the last straw. Dayan approved a response, although he had initially opposed invading and occupying the West Bank. But as the Egyptian army in Sinai disintegrated after only three days of mopping up operations following the initial breakthroughs, he allowed Israeli forces to strike east as well.

The campaign on the West Bank was the exact opposite of the ferocious and heartbreaking struggles there in 1947–1948. Then the Arab Legion had proven more than a match for anything the amateurish and newly cobbled together Israeli forces could throw at them. Every Israeli

Too Good to Be True?

On that first, extraordinary day of the 1967 war, Michael Elkins, the CBS Radio News correspondent in Israel, filed an apparently sensational but accurate account of the extent of Israel's initial victory. It sounded so ludicrous to the suits in Manhattan that they refused to air it. The British Broadcasting Corporation, for whom Elkins also worked, proved more sensible. They broadcast his report, which is how the British learned about Israel's rout of the Egyptians before the Americans did.

The only comparable military strike in history was the annihilation of the Soviet Air Force by the Luftwaffe on June 22, 1941, at the beginning of Operation Barbarossa, Hitler's invasion of Russia. And as happened on that occasion, once the Egyptians' air umbrella was wiped out, their huge ground forces proved to be sitting ducks for the superbly coordinated Israeli blitzkrieg tactics that hit them.

offensive operation against the Legion forces in 1948 failed. In 1967, every one of them succeeded. The Arab Legion was still excellently trained and led. Of all the Arab forces, they fought the longest, hardest, and best in that war and inflicted the most casualties on the Israeli army. But they were outnumbered, out-equipped, out-trained, and at an operational level entirely out-soldiered. The Old City of Jerusalem fell to Israeli forces and the rest of the West Bank did as well.

Finally, Dayan was determined to end nineteen years of bombardments of Israeli settlements in the far north from the Syrian forces on the supposedly impregnable Golan Heights. In 1948 and again in 1967, the Syrian army proved totally incapable of any serious attacks whatsoever. Though Syrian soldiers fought hard in their defensive positions, they had no operational or tactical solutions to the Israeli armored juggernaut. Israel took the Golan Heights, just as it took the West Bank and Sinai. In six days, Israel's enemies had been routed on three major battle fronts. Israeli forces had swept to the Suez Canal, and the Old City of Jerusalem was suddenly in Jewish hands for the first time in more than two thousand years.

The war was a stunning humiliation not only for Nasser but for the Soviet Union, which had poured so much military hardware into Egypt and Syria. The point was not lost on the American public and on policy-makers in Washington.

Results of the Six-Day War

The Six-Day War did not create today's Middle East. The region has been through plenty more changes—some of them far bloodier—since then. But the war certainly transformed the region. Israel suddenly appeared not as an idealized little state teetering on the brink of destruction but as a regional military superpower, a kosher version of Sparta. The state itself was also transformed by the war. Its citizens grew proud and far more macho. While justly proud of their citizen-army and its amazing prowess, they started developing a widespread contempt for Arab military capabilities. That attitude would cost them dearly in another war only six years later.

For the first time Israel had conquered territories to administer and develop. Levi Eshkol, Golda Meir, and Yitzhak Rabin, the three Labor Party prime ministers who inherited what Israeli author Shabtai Tevet called the "cursed blessing," tried to prevent significant Jewish settlement in those territories. They wanted to retain control, primarily for security reasons, but as far as possible to let the Palestinians there handle their own affairs.

The war also transformed the existential nature of Israel. Throughout the twentieth century, the Jewish community in Palestine had grown. The socialist democracy Ben-Gurion had created and led gave a lot of legal protection and special rights to the originally small Orthodox Jewish minority, but that had been granted on the comfortable secular assumption that the unworldly religious would stay in their own corner and probably quietly assimilate into the general population. Instead, they flourished and grew at a rapid pace.

In the Arab world, every major Arab leader whose country fought in the war—Egypt, Jordan, Syria, and Iraq—was toppled within three years, with the exception of Jordan's King Hussein. Syria and Iraq became stronger Soviet allies under the more stable (and brutal) Ba'ath Arab socialist dictatorships, with torturer and hit man Saddam Hussein coming to effective power in Baghdad in 1968 and former air force chief Hafez Assad taking power in Damascus in 1970.

At first, Nasser thought he could continue to lead the Arab world by spearheading its hostility toward Israel, as he had before. He organized a massive pan-Arab, anti-Zionist conference in Khartoum, the capital of Sudan. He rapidly rebuilt his army and air force with his Soviet backers. By 1969, he felt strong enough to start bombarding the defenses the Israelis had built to hold the eastern bank of the Suez Canal. In so doing, he launched the War of Attrition. It proved to be the last and in some respects the most costly of all his bungles.

The Israelis had now a lot more power to respond to Nasser's provocations than they had had back in the 1950s. Israeli aircraft devastated the cities on the canal's western shore, the most sophisticated and most prosperous in Egypt. In a few months, the poorest country in the Middle East was carrying the additional burden of half a million refugees. Nasser as a politician was finished long before he died of a heart attack at the age of fifty-two. He looked and acted as if he were twenty years older.

Nixon: Israel's best friend

In 1968, Levi Eshkol sent Lieutenant General Yitzhak Rabin to Washington as Israel's ambassador in order to get him out of the way. He was a

PC Myth: The U.S. Backed Israel from Birth

The United States has not always been Israel's protector and shield. In fact, successive U.S. governments, while passively sympathetic to the Jewish state, regarded it generally as an embarrassment and kept it at arm's length for the first twenty years of its existence.

Democratic president Harry S Truman, privately the most virulent anti-Semite ever to sit in the Oval Office, later claimed to be a warm, appreciative friend of Israel, but in office he wasn't. Truman's two secretaries of state, George Marshall and Dean Acheson, certainly weren't. Truman did not lift a finger to provide any significant official U.S. military or civilian aid to Israel. The skies of the early Jewish state were protected by Nazi-designed Messerschmitt Bf-109s built in and sold by Czechoslovakia, a Soviet satellite. France, not the United States, was the Western democracy that first came to Israel's aid and sold it the aircraft and tanks it desperately needed.

Meanwhile, the cost of absorbing, feeding, and clothing the hundreds of thousands of Jewish refugees suddenly kicked out of major Arab nations like Iraq, Egypt, and Yemen was crushing. And the State of Israel, with only 1.5 million people, almost half of them destitute refugees, had no money to buy the modern weapons it urgently needed to defend itself. Rescue for the infant Jewish state came from the last direction anyone would have expected.

At first, President Dwight D. Eisenhower and his secretary of state, John Foster Dulles, weren't Israel's friends either. They cracked down hard on Israel in the 1956 Suez crisis. But when Israel deterred Syria from invading Jordan in 1958 as U.S. Marines were landing in Lebanon to prevent a horrendous civil

continued on next page

continued from previous page

war, Eisenhower and Dulles realized the Israelis not only could take care of themselves, but could handle other potential problems in the region as well. Relations became a lot warmer after that.

The seeds of what would become a major secret alliance between America's CIA and the Israeli Mossad were laid in the mid-1950s. The key figures in creating it were James Jesus Angleton, the legendary and eventually paranoid CIA counter-intelligence chief, and Teddy Kollek, a close friend of David Ben-Gurion.

Relations improved significantly when John F. Kennedy entered the White House. Kennedy's father, Joseph Kennedy, had been an outspoken anti-Semite in the 1930s and 1940s and became notorious as ambassador to Britain in the first years of World War II. The elder Kennedy regarded Winston Churchill with contempt and thought Nazi Germany would defeat the British in 1940. But his son proved to be a very different kind of man.

JFK sold Hawk anti-aircraft missiles—the best weapons system of its kind in the world at the time—to Israel. And after tough old pro-Israeli West German chancellor Konrad Adenauer retired in 1963, Kennedy kept pressure on Adenauer's far weaker successor, Ludwig Erhard, to honor Adenauer's pledge to sell U.S.-built Patton tanks to Israel. Those tanks proved of great importance to Israel in winning its stunning Six-Day War victory.

Kennedy's successor, Lyndon Johnson, was also sympathetic to Israel, but he was too preoccupied with the Vietnam War to be active in the Middle East—though he certainly welcomed the setback for Soviet power in the region from Israel's Six-Day War victory. But it was only under President Richard Nixon that the United States tilted decisively in favor of supporting Israel.

war hero and therefore a political threat to Eshkol and to Golda Meir, who would succeed Eshkol as prime minister. The post of envoy to Washington in those days was still seen as something of a backwater. France had been Israel's main supporter and supplier of arms, especially aircraft, since the creation of the state. The United States was seen as important more for the private fund-raising from its Jewish community, the largest and wealthiest in the world, than for its strategic relationship.

Things changed rapidly after Rabin arrived in Washington. First, President Charles de Gaulle of France, who had always had something of a latent contempt for Jews (he had served closely with General Philippe Petain after World War I) became furious at Israel for going to war to save itself in 1967 rather than heed his call for restraint. De Gaulle first made some notorious public slurs against Jews at a presidential press conference, and then he followed up his words with action by imposing an arms embargo on Israel. The arms embargo came just as the Soviet Union, pouring good money after bad, was sending even more new arms, especially state-of-the-art aircraft, to Egypt, Iraq, and Syria. And Israel was running out of spare parts for its precious Dassault Mirage IIIs. To add insult to injury, with de Gaulle's blessing, the Dassault company began selling Mirages to Arab nations like Iraq and Libya. Britain under Harold Wilson was generally sympathetic to Israel but unwilling to incur Arab anger by selling it advanced arms. And besides, the British at that time had no fighter-bomber to compare with the Mirage. The United States did, in its superb McDonnell Douglas F-4 Phantom.

In January 1969, Lyndon Johnson stepped down as president, worn out by the Vietnam War, race riots, and the chaotic antiwar rage on America's college campuses. His successor, Richard Nixon, was already a friend and admirer of Rabin's.

When Nixon visited Israel in the 1960s, his political career seemed to be over after his defeat in California's gubernatorial race. Rabin was then chief of staff of the Israel Defense Forces, and he gave the former U.S.

vice president the red-carpet treatment. A touched Nixon remained forever grateful.

As Nixon became president of the United States, so Golda Meir became prime minister of Israel. With Egypt continuing to wage its War of Attrition along the Suez Canal, and with Israeli air superiority in increasing doubt, even Meir realized how important relations with the United States had become. Besides, the one thing Meir, raised in Milwaukee, was good at was talking to Americans. She hit it off with Nixon from the word go. Beneath her lovable grandmother veneer, of course, she was as tough, uncompromising, hard-headed, mean, selfish, and vicious as he was. He liked that.

While historians and the media like to paint Richard Nixon as a hateful anti-Semite (and he certainly had his prejudices), it's undeniable that he saved Israel in 1973. The crucial C-5A Galaxy airlift that Nixon authorized and Defense Secretary James Schlesinger brilliantly implemented at breakneck speed saved Israel during the Yom Kippur War. It also brought home to Israeli policymakers how crucial the United States had become to ensuring the very survival of their state. Thirty-five years later, that lesson still holds good.

1973: The Israelis mess up big

The 1973 Yom Kippur War, or War of Ramadan, began as a direct contrast to the 1967 Six-Day War. And as such, it was a sobering lesson of how quickly national fates can change, winners become losers, and despised incompetents transform themselves into formidable threats.

After the 1967 war, the Israeli army became complacent and arrogant, reinforced by the fact that at a tactical level, the Israelis won every skirmish, battle, and commando operation in the War of Attrition from 1969 to 1970. In 1970, they even stole an entire Soviet-built radar station from the Egyptians. But Egypt came out of the War of Attrition with one long-term strategic advantage. The Israeli air force had not been able to dislodge a new generation of Soviet-made ground-to-air missiles along the west side of the Suez Canal. More important was the evolution in Egyptian equipment and combat tactics that took place after the 1967 war. Egypt's new president, Anwar Sadat, who came to power in 1970, transformed Egypt's military leadership, including elevating Air Marshal Hosni Mubarak to chief of staff of the air force. Mubarak and General Ahmad Ismail Ali (appointed war minister) and General Saad al-Shazli (appointed army commander in chief) carefully analyzed the catastrophic defeat of 1967. They took seriously the scathing internal criticisms from senior officers in the Egyptian army. They clearly recognized the need to neutralize the Israeli superiority in pilots and tank crews and to equip large numbers of their ground troops with the Soviets' cheap new mass-produced anti-tank missiles. They were not political plotters and intriguers like Nasser's favorites and cronies. Ismail Ali and Shazli in particular later fell afoul of Sadat, opposing his more moderate policies toward Israel. They and other officers were expelled from power, jailed, or exiled. Mubarak, who remained quietly loyal, succeeded Sadat as president and ruled Egypt as well as anyone could for more than a quarter of a century. All three men were intelligent, energetic, analytical, and possessed of great professional integrity. They were light years away from the arrogant, posturing Field Marshal Abdel Hakim Amer, who had led the Egyptian army to shameful humiliation twice in the 1956 and 1967 wars. And unlike Amer, they learned well the lessons of defeat and put them to good use, as the Israelis soon learned to their cost.

Shazli trained the Egyptian army to undertake careful, limited-range offensives under the protection of the new surface-to-air anti-aircraft missile screen from the Soviets. He and his staff painstakingly developed defensive tactics using their new missiles against Israeli massed tank attacks. He did not blindly flood the Egyptian army with showy high-tech Soviet weapons and then neglect to train his soldiers in effective combat

Israeli Cyclops

The Israeli army didn't start out as the invincible juggernaut it would become. One man made the difference: the abrasive, one-eyed loner Moshe Dayan, whom Prime Minister David Ben-Gurion raised to chief of staff of the Israeli army, ignoring senior left-wing officers in the top leadership. Dayan taught the infant army a radically new combat ethos. He insisted on the ruthless attainment of combat objectives, regardless of casualties; retaliatory attacks against Arab terrorists (which horrified dovish Israeli politicians); shock attacks made at night and via indirect approaches; junior officers and ordinary soldiers seizing the initiative in the field; and combat training that was far tougher than it had been. Dayan's command style owed a lot, ironically, to that of Panzer General Heinz Guderian, who developed the idea of the *Blitzkrieg*. The modern image of the Israeli soldier as informal, arrogant, and unbeatable comes from Dayan.

tactics with them, as Amer had. Shazli made sure his soldiers were equipped only with weapons that were well within their technological capabilities. He gave them a new generation of small wire-guided anti-tank missiles and ground-to-air anti-aircraft missiles. He also worked hard on planning how to cross the Suez Canal in overwhelming force and retake the east bank, where Israel had erected apparently impregnable new defenses: the Bar-Lev Line.

Dayan objected to the new line, and once again his instincts were sound. But he became an increasingly passive figure as minister of defense in the five-year buildup to the Yom Kippur War. Originally, Dayan had not wanted the Israeli army to sweep all the way to the Suez Canal. And then he certainly had not wanted to maintain Israel's front line of defense on it. (If the stories about Dayan participating in the

Dnieper crossing, the greatest amphibious operation in history against a hostile defended shore in terms of combat troops involved, are correct, he had seen shore defenses vastly more impressive than the Bar-Lev Line smashed.)

But Dayan was outflanked. He could not get his own way with Golda Meir, and he had already acquiesced in the disastrous appointment of Lieutenant General Chaim Bar-Lev, a Labor Party loyalist, as chief of staff in 1968.

Bar-Lev was far more rigid, arrogant, and doctrinaire than the informal Dayan or the shy, low-key, but exceptionally intelligent and analytical workaholic Yitzhak Rabin. He was convinced he had the answers to everything. His family originated in the Yugoslav Jewish community, as did that of his protégé and successor Lieutenant General David Elazar. Bar-Lev and Elazar, unlike Dayan, Ariel Sharon, and Rabin, put their faith in static defenses. They did not heed the warning of George S. Patton that static defenses are a lasting monument to the stupidity of man. They thought the Arabs were useless, that Israel could sit back in its mighty new defenses and massacre its enemies at will. The Israeli army had fallen into the hands of generals who wanted to revive the Maginot Line.

But the Bar-Lev Line was a hollow shell. First, unlike the far more formidable Siegfried and Maginot Lines during World War II, it wasn't a line at all. It was a series of separate strongholds constructed along the Suez Canal, each supposedly able to give the others covering fire. Second, the whole idea of the line was that it required soldiers and significant mobilized reserve forces to man it.

But before the Egyptian attack finally came on October 6, 1973, Prime Minister Meir, despite many warnings, had flatly refused to call up any reserves. She was convinced the attack would never come. In the event, a few hundred Israeli army soldiers, mostly regular conscripts doing their three-year tour of duty, were hit head-on by an Egyptian army of 80,000 men. The massive amphibious operation to cross the canal had been prepared meticulously and it went off like a dream. Meir and Bar-Lev's strategic conception evaporated in a matter of hours.

Even worse lay in store for the Israelis. The mobilized Israeli army rolled into the Sinai Peninsula to scatter the Egyptians as they had done three times before—in 1948, 1956, and 1967. But this was a very different Egyptian army. It had been excellently trained and drilled and this time it was prepared for the kind of attacks it was going to face. The new cheap, easily produced, anti-tank and anti-aircraft missiles that it deployed changed the face of war. The previously invincible Israeli tanks were knocked out by the score, eventually by the hundreds. The first Israeli counter-attacks were launched far too soon without remotely sufficient planning. The personnel choices of Bar-Lev and Elazar as senior front commanders proved uniformly disastrous—a striking contrast to Dayan and Rabin, who as chiefs of staff had both been outstanding judges of men. The Israelis in their first attacks even made the same elementary errors that had cost the British and Soviet armies so heavily against the Wehrmacht in 1941 and 1942. They counter-attacked with tanks in massed formation without first clearing the way with infantry assault troops. As a result, the tanks were sitting ducks for heavy anti-tank weapons and infantry armed with handheld anti-tank weapons.

A week into the war, with Israel's first counter-attacks smashed and ammunition and weapons reserves running dangerously low, the Jewish state was in greater danger of being overrun by the Egyptians than it had been in 1948 or 1967. In the 1956 and 1967 wars, the Israeli air force had served as flying artillery after quickly and apparently easily winning command of the skies. Consequently, the Israeli army had never invested in heavy artillery. It cost too much and slowed down the fast-moving army. And who needed it when the air force could do the job better anyway?

But in 1973, the Israeli air force could no longer do the job. The Egyptians' new surface-to-air missiles saw to that. There was a turkey shoot of Israel's elite pilots and expensive aircraft.

With Syria and Iraq attacking from the north and Egypt moving rapidly across Sinai, Israel looked to be imperiled. Supporting the Arab states were the Soviet Union, Saudi Arabia, Kuwait, Morocco, Libya, Algeria, Tunisia, Sudan, the Palestinians, and even Pakistan and Cuba.

Two things eventually saved Israel from disaster. The first was the great C5-A Galaxy airlift, dubbed Operation Nickel Grass. It was one of the largest, quickest, most successful emergency resupply operations the U.S. Air Force had ever carried out. Many of America's NATO allies refused to let the aircraft land for refueling, but the Portuguese government helped save the Jewish state by allowing the U.S. to use the Lajes air base on the Azores islands in the western Atlantic.

The second factor that turned defeat into victory in the south was the man who inherited Dayan's old mantle as Israel's greatest combat commander: General Ariel Sharon. He had been squeezed out of the army into early retirement and had immediately turned his boundless energies into transforming domestic politics, convincing the notoriously small-thinking Menachem Begin to expand his free-market, right-wing coalition into a far broader nationalist coalition—the Likud bloc. Now restored to military command, he worked a similar transformation on the battlefield, leading Israeli tanks to thwart the Egyptian thrust and turn the tide against what could have been a disaster for Israel.

Resupplied and under reinvigorated leadership, the Israelis drove the Arabs back to the point that the Syrian and Egyptian regimes felt that they—no longer the Israelis—were in danger of collapse.

Results of the 1973 war

In 1967, a miraculous, overwhelming Israeli victory at low cost led to more war. In 1973, a far more ferocious war costing almost four times as many lives led to more than thirty years of peace with the two Arab antagonists.

Both Israel and the major Arab combat states were greatly sobered by the war. The Israelis learned that they could not underestimate the military capabilities of neighboring Arab states. Once the hard-headed and rather brainless Golda Meir was forced out of power, a younger, much more pragmatic generation of Israeli leaders ready to make political compromises with the Arabs took over. It is telling that the greatest territorial concessions were given by the supposedly most right-wing and intransigent Israeli leader of them all, Menachem Begin, when he returned the entire Sinai Peninsula to Egypt by 1981. The major Arab nations had learned a lesson as well. Egypt and Syria had caught the Israeli army totally by surprise. Their weapons and combat tactics, especially those of the Egyptian infantry in the first week of the war, were vastly superior. For the first time in any war, they had even inflicted a tactical defeat on the Israeli air force and prevented it from providing decisive tactical support to Israeli ground forces. Yet despite all these advantages, the Arab armies still lost, and the cease-fires in the north and south came with Israeli combat forces on both fronts poised to take Damascus and Cairo.

Senior leaders in Egypt and Syria remained in power for three decades after the war, and in both countries they took those lessons very much to heart. Syrian president Hafez Assad held power for another twenty-seven years until his death in 2000. His defense minister Mustafa Tlass stayed in power until 2004. Despite their openly expressed ferocious anti-Semitism and ugly record of torturing and killing Israeli prisoners of war in 1973, neither of them ever dared risk breaking the Golan Heights armistice by killing a single Israeli soldier on that front as long as they lived.

And in Egypt, air force chief of staff Mubarak, who performed so outstandingly before and during the war, remains president of Egypt in 2007 after taking power in 1981. And so far he has never risked breaking the 1979 Israel-Egypt peace treaty.

Chapter 7

THE SAUDIS ARE PART OF THE SOLUTION, NOT THE PROBLEM

The enemy of my enemy is my friend

Michael Moore's *Fahrenheit 9/11* seems to argue that the Saudi royal family are the real bad guys in the Arab world. When you consider Saudi Arabia's history, that seems odd. Of all the Arab nations, Saudi Arabia has the greatest chance of bringing peace and stability to the region. Historically, the Saudis have been on our side more often than any other Arab nation. But when you look at them through the lens of lefty political correctness, it makes sense:

- ◎ Elements of the Saudi royal family have a diplomatic, personal, and professional relationship with the Bush family. This is proof enough to many that they are evil.
- ◎ Saudi Arabia's economy is based on oil, which, as we all know, is evil.
- ◎ Saudi Arabia's leaders are devoutly religious, but they don't hate America.

The oil connection

The kingdom of Saudi Arabia has been the largest and most lucrative partner of major U.S. oil companies in the world for seventy-five years. During that time, U.S. oil companies have prospered from the partnership, as

Guess what?

- ❀ In the Islamic Middle East, repressive rule works; religious liberty doesn't.
- ❀ The Saudis have the right enemies: al Qaeda and Michael Moore.
- ❀ September 11 was a plot against the Saudis too.
- ❀ We couldn't have beaten Communism without the Saudis.

have U.S. national interests. Since 1967, Saudi Arabia has been the world's crucial "swing" producer of oil. That means it is the one country with such enormous and easily accessible oil reserves that it can affect global oil prices more than any other nation by increasing or decreasing production and sales.

From 1933 to 1973, Saudi oil flowed to the United States at bargain-basement prices. After the 1973 Yom Kippur War, the Saudis joined forces with the shah of Iran (Richard Nixon's favorite despot) to quadruple global oil prices. But even then, the Saudis did not use their huge new revenues to undermine or oppose the United States; they invested the lion's share of the money in America.

In the 1980s, U.S.-Saudi relations became more important than ever. King Fahd took the throne in 1982 after the death of his brother King Khaled, but he had been the real power in the kingdom since the assassination of King Faisal in 1975. Fahd loved America and was convinced the Saudis needed U.S. protection from the Soviet Union, Iran, and other potential threatening powers. Fahd stepped up the already close cooper-

Local Boy Done Good

"In order to be a leader of men, a man has to receive an education in his own country, among his own people, and to grow up in surroundings steeped with the traditions and psychology of his countrymen. Not only did Western education not fulfill that condition, but it tended to wean a young man from the customs and traditions of his country."

King Abdulaziz ibn Saud, as quoted by Charles Crane, 1931, and as cited by Ronald Lacey in *The Kingdom: Arabia and the House of Saud*

ation with the Reagan administration to fund the mujahedin guerrillas who were fighting the Red Army to a standstill in Afghanistan. Saudi willingness to keep global oil prices low was also a major reason for the terminal crisis that toppled the Soviet Union in the 1980s. The Soviets then (like Russia now) was dependent on profits from its oil and gas exports to stay afloat. The Saudi role in toppling communism was therefore arguably greater even than those of major U.S. allies like Britain, Germany, and Japan. They were friends when we needed them to be.

In 2002, King Abdullah ibn Abdulaziz changed the nation's energy pricing policy: the Saudis became committed to stable higher oil prices rather than stable lower ones. They needed the extra money to buy prosperity (and thus peace and security) at home. The rising threat of Iran across the Gulf unnerved them. And with China's thirst for oil growing by leaps and bounds, and Japan, South Korea, and India not far behind, the pressure to keep global prices high and output low was growing. But even then, the Saudis were determined not to kill the goose that laid the golden eggs: the health of the global economy.

The biggest bottleneck in global oil supplies is the dearth of oil refineries around the world, especially in the United States. Successive American administrations, Republican and Democrat alike, have blithely ignored this fact. Most major international oil companies have concentrated on paying their healthy profit margins to their shareholders; they haven't invested in new refinery infrastructure. The only major exception to this rule in recent years has been Saudi-owned Aramco. Once again the Saudis turned out to be the responsible good guys, though you wouldn't know it by listening to the fevered Left, who seem to think the Saudis are the only bad Arabs.

Saudi Arabia has, in absolute numbers, the largest and wealthiest middle class in the Arab world. A large, stable, propertied middle class is the essential prerequisite for any country's successful transition to a healthy democracy in the long term. That was as true for England in the eighteenth and nineteenth centuries as it was for South Korea and Malaysia in the twentieth century.

It was obviously better for America when Texas was our chief source of oil, but our own endless thirst for "Texas tea" drank the Texas gushers dry. Suppose Saudi Arabia's wells ran dry or the kingdom was torn apart. Who could replace it as the world's next dominant "swing" producer?

There are only two real candidates: Iraq and Russia. Iraq has five enormous fields south of Baghdad that haven't even begun to be developed yet. Russia under President Vladimir Putin is already the world's number-two exporter of crude oil after the Saudis and the number-one exporter of natural gas and oil combined. And if you think the American people and the national interests of the United States would be better served by switching from the Saudis to the Kremlin or Baghdad, Michael Moore may love you, but nobody else will.

Michael Moore's mania:
The Saudis were behind September 11

This "Big Lie" worthy of Joseph Goebbels has probably been the most successful and destructive myth to come out of the September 11 atrocities. The simple and obvious truth is that Osama bin Laden, a renegade from one of Saudi Arabia's wealthiest and most respected families, deliberately selected as many Saudi nationals as he could to hijack the four airliners and carry out the attacks because he wanted to destroy Saudi Arabia's close ties with the United States. He came a lot closer to succeeding than most people realize.

It was true that up to September 11, the Saudis had complacently tolerated the most extreme anti-American and anti-Israeli sentiments being taught in their mosques, and they took no efforts to crack down on them. Even after the attacks, this state of affairs continued for another year. The

Saudis assumed that al Qaeda and similar groups would not attack them if they gave them no offense.

This policy was not unique to al Qaeda, and it did not mean the Saudis in any way sympathized with al Qaeda's aims. After all, al Qaeda's aims were very explicitly the destruction of the Saudi monarchy and its replacement with an extremist caliphate that controlled Saudi oil reserves and the two most holy places in the Muslim world, Mecca and Medina, both of which lie in Saudi territory.

But the Saudis wanted a quiet kingdom and were prepared to pay or look the other way in order to get it. September 11 should have been a wake-up call to the Saudi government to crack down on its own extremist preachers and on the danger of al Qaeda establishing itself in the desert kingdom. But for twenty months after the attacks, the Saudis were relatively blasé about the threat bin Laden posed to his own home country.

That changed on May 12, 2003, when nine al Qaeda suicide bombers attacked a Riyadh residential compound where Westerners were living, killing twenty-six people. Al Qaeda had shown its determination to topple Saudi Arabia. It proved to be a big mistake

Why separation of mosque and state is folly

To their credit, the Saudis, under the able energetic direction of King Abdullah, woke up fast. The way they handled the immediate threat from al Qaeda over the next four years has been almost ignored in the American media. But it is an object lesson in the sensible and successful ways in which Middle East Arab governments can defeat such murderous and nihilistic groups.

First, the Saudis recognized the need to tackle the problem at its source. They started monitoring sermons given in mosques throughout the kingdom by *qadis*, local religious leaders and preachers. Extreme Islamists who espoused al Qaeda's wild goals or preached sedition against the Riyadh government were identified and removed from their positions. The worst ones were expelled from the country. The Saudis also instituted a gradual but increasingly effective policy of imposing state control over religious institutions and teachers of Islam to marginalize and discredit Islamist leaders. This policy was studied and copied with great success by Russian president Vladimir Putin. Indeed, Britain was the only major country that allowed radical Islamists to preach their extremism unmolested. The Saudis found themselves in the ironic position of privately asking, in vain, Prime Minister Tony Blair and the British security services to muzzle the radicals. On July 7, 2005, the British learned the price of not heeding the Saudis' warnings.

The British weakness resulted from the wish to apply Western standards to the Muslim world—a widespread folly since September 11, and the same one the British had committed in their empire days. In Judeo-Christian countries, church and state ought to leave one another alone. After hundreds of years of wrangling, that is standard practice in the Christian West, and is thoroughly in accord with what Jesus taught in the gospels: render unto Caesar that which is Caesar's and unto God that which is God's. But Islam doesn't leave the state alone, and so the state can't leave it alone. In fact, the control of religious leaders, down to mosque level, has always been a traditional function of every Muslim government.

The Ottoman Empire specialized in controlling the mosques, which is why they held on so well for so long. When the naïve British didn't kill or exile the mufti of Jerusalem, Haj Amin al-Husseini, in the 1920s and 1930s, they allowed him to spread his doctrine of murderous violence. As the mufti was allowed to preach, the Palestinian Arab population concluded (not unreasonably) that the British approved of him. After the 2003 bombings, the Saudis didn't make the same mistake.

The Saudis also unleashed their own domestic security services in ways that made the Bush administration's domestic response to September 11 seem liberal and wimpy. And far from being corrupt, sympathetic to the terrorists, or incapable, the Saudi forces responded superbly.

How to fight Muslim terrorists: Build walls and monitor the mosques

Ignored by virtually the entire American domestic media, the Saudi security campaign against al Qaeda from 2002 through 2006 proved to be a total success, in marked contrast to the fiascos unfolding next door in Iraq.

In those years, to be promoted to the position of al Qaeda commander or director of operations in Saudi Arabia was a guaranteed death sentence. The Saudis killed half a dozen of them in a row.

By 2005, the Saudis were building state-of-the-art, high-tech security barriers along their borders with Yemen to the south and Iraq to the northeast. These systems were inspired by the success of former Israeli prime minister Ariel Sharon's security fence, which proved to be the decisive weapon in beating the bloody suicide bomber onslaught of the second Palestinian Intifada.

Also, albeit belatedly, the Saudis started to monitor and rewrite their own traditional school textbooks to remove passages that would give aid, comfort, and legitimacy to al Qaeda sympathizers.

It also helped that soaring oil prices in the first decade of the twenty-first century came as a new windfall for Saudi Arabia. King Abdullah's 1999 accord with Iran to boost global oil prices had worked extremely well.

The Saudis and Arafat: From appeasement to realism

The original Saudi policy of accommodation toward al Qaeda was not admirable, but it was a far cry from eagerly supporting the terror group, let alone cooperating in its September 11 attacks on the United States. It was consistent with the decades-old Saudi policies of accommodation toward Yasser Arafat and his Palestine Liberation Organization.

For more than a quarter of a century, the Saudis paid the PLO huge sums of protection money so Arafat and his guerrillas would leave them alone. But even that policy didn't last forever.

In 1990, after Saddam Hussein conquered Kuwait and looked poised to conquer Saudi Arabia, Arafat eagerly jumped on Saddam's bandwagon and offered his support. The Saudis were furious, and they finally cut the PLO off and cracked down on its operations and fund-raising. Because Arafat was so cash-starved and weakened by this Saudi reaction, he put on a more moderate face and agreed to Israeli foreign minister Shimon Peres's proposals to enter the 1993 Oslo Peace Process.

Understanding the Saudis

In short, while sometimes short-sighted, the Saudis have nevertheless sided with the West more often than not. To fully understand the Saudi psyche requires, of course, delving into their history. For our purposes, we need only go back to World War I, when Saudi Arabia and the West became fully intertwined.

A little Saudi history: The myth of Lawrence of Arabia

T. E. Lawrence, known as Lawrence of Arabia, had an enormous impact on Western conceptions of the Arab world. He even advised Winston Churchill in drawing up what became the map of the modern Middle East at the Cairo Conference of 1921. But he was never the great benefactor and liberator of the Arab peoples his admirers made him out to be. He was a potentially talented archaeologist, a writer and self-dramatizer of extraordinary genius, and a wildly unstable individual with a bewildering variety of highly entertaining fetishes. He was, however, far from the prophet of the Arab Awakening he imagined himself to be, and he was a military genius only in his own dreams.

In his wonderful book *Seven Pillars of Wisdom* (best read as a highly colored work of pure fiction) Lawrence presents the Arab revolt in the desert as a national uprising ignored by the pedantic British authorities in Cairo but fanned by him. In his telling, it was the crucial episode of World War I in the Middle East, destroying all Ottoman power throughout the Arabian peninsula.

In reality, the revolt was made possible only by enormous British subsidies and bribes paid to the Hashemite family, led by Sherif Hussein, who was the hereditary guardian of the Muslim holy places in Mecca. But Sherif Hussein was despised and distrusted by the general population of the Hejaz, the Red Sea coast region of Arabia, and his writ never ran inside the desert vastness of the Arabian peninsula, where the dynamic young Abdulaziz ibn Saud was then already master of all he surveyed. The tribesmen Lawrence was able to bribe or buy, who agreed to work with him on behalf of the sherif and his sons, did carry out their famous raid on Aqaba. But this was a tiny sideshow militarily irrelevant to the huge clash of the British and Ottoman imperial armies of more than 70,000 men each in the 1917–1918 battles for Palestine.

In 1920, at the urging of British political officials, British military commanders quietly withdrew their forces from the Syrian capital of Damascus, in order to clear the way for its fictional liberation by Hashemite Arab forces. This was a

Peter O'Toole Could Make *Anyone* Look Good

"Lawrence's record, then, shows bravery in war, a great capacity for physical endurance, ingenuity as a guerrilla leader, and later some literary talent. But it also shows that he was self-centered, mercurial, and violently unstable."

Elie Kedourie, "Colonel Lawrence and His Biographers," in *Islam in the Modern World*

clumsy attempt to undermine the French authorities from occupying Syria in accord with their previous agreements with Britain, and to foster the myth that the British were the champions of Arab nationalism while the French were its cruel enemies. The French treated the British ploy with contempt. A Pan-Arab congress did meet in Damascus in 1920 until the occupying French expelled it. Lawrence, in *Seven Pillars of Wisdom*, did more than any other single person to establish the myth that the British had evicted the Ottomans (thanks to the Arabs) and had then betrayed the nationalist movement they launched. This interpretation was eagerly adopted by generations of British anti-colonial intellectuals and was a leitmotif of the Royal Institute for International Affairs at Chatham House in London for around half a century, creating what the late historian Elie Kedourie called in a famous essay "The Chatham House Version" of modern Middle Eastern history.

In reality, Arab nationalism grew in the great cities of Cairo, Baghdad, and Damascus, and it was fueled by a perfectly understandable and

Bin Laden on Saudi Arabia

Was the Saudi regime behind September 11? In contrast, Osama bin Laden founded al Qaeda as a reaction against Saudi Arabia's pro-America leanings. Here's an excerpt from an interview bin Laden did with CNN's Peter Arnett in March 1997:

> The Saudi regime is but a branch or an agent of the U.S. By being loyal to the U.S. regime, the Saudi regime has committed an act against Islam. And this, based on the ruling of *sharia*, casts the regime outside the religious community. Subsequently, the regime has stopped ruling people according to what Allah revealed, praise and glory be to Him, not to mention many other contradictory acts. When this main foundation was violated, other corrupt acts followed in every aspect of the country, the economic, the social, government services and so on.

straightforward resentment of British and French occupation of the great territories of Egypt and what became modern Syria and Iraq.

Far from being a visionary prophet for the Arabs, Lawrence was a classic example of an alienated young adventurer who projected his own fantasies onto a foreign people he did not understand and who understandably had little time for him. He had zero effect on the history and growth of Arab nationalism.

Everything he did, for the most bizarre and selfish reasons, seemed to feed his legend. He abandoned his fame to serve as a humble airman in the British Royal Air Force under an assumed name. He got uneducated young airmen to whip him and to otherwise physically abuse him. He even had them write reports about his reactions to being tortured so that he could read them afterward. He was killed in a motorcycle accident in 1935. Given the way he rode his bike at high speed through the narrow English country lanes, the only surprise was it had not happened years earlier. Needless to say, conspiracy theories eventually swirled around his demise. Had he lived, he might well have wrought more mischief and chaos with the schemes he would have whispered into Churchill's ear during World War II. In the 1960s, a superb movie starring Peter O'Toole revived Lawrence's allure. O'Toole was tall, amazingly handsome, and irresistible to the ladies. Lawrence was none of those things. He was short, coyly intellectual-looking with a large nose in an oval face, and found the female form repulsive.

His enduring reputation confirms the idea that old legends, like old soldiers, never die. But unlike old soldiers, legends like Lawrence's don't fade away; they just come back with more allure and fantasy than ever.

The Arab revolt that worked

The real Arab revolt was led by Abdulaziz ibn Saud. The contrasts between Ibn Saud and Lawrence, and with Lawrence's icons Sherif Hussein of

Mecca and his younger son Faisal, were profound. Ibn Saud was a real prince, a man of action and a warrior hero. With his family he fled Riyadh and went into exile when he was only a teenager. In the Arabian heartland, he showed political as well as military genius in merging his loyal Bedouin tribes with the Wahhabi purists of the Islamic faith. He led what amounted to both an Arab nationalist and Islamic fundamentalist restoration movement. Its austerity, integrity, and sense of justice made it popular, and by 1914 he was the master of the Arabian heartland, a desert almost as large as India.

During World War I, Ibn Saud prudently steered clear of both the British and the Ottomans. He did not like or trust the secular Young Turk radicals who had seized control of the great empire in 1908, and though advised and subsidized by the British, he took his own course. In the 1920s, he completed his conquest of Arabia by sending his forces to capture the two holiest cities in Islam, Mecca and Medina.

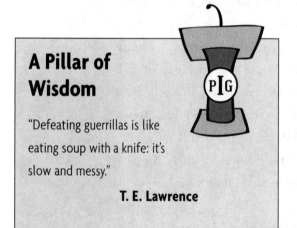

A Pillar of Wisdom

"Defeating guerrillas is like eating soup with a knife: it's slow and messy."

T. E. Lawrence

Mecca and Medina were run by Sherif Hussein, the British idol Sir Henry McMahon and Sir Ronald Storrs had so ardently wooed in their infamous and bungled 1915 McMahon-Hussein letters. And Lawrence and Gertrude Bell had worked so hard and so well to present Hussein's son Faisal as a great warrior-prince and statesman to David Lloyd George and Winston Churchill.

But in reality, Sherif Hussein was despised and resented as a repressive, greedy bumbler by his long-suffering subjects. Not only could the Hashemites not set the Arab Muslim world aflame against the Ottomans, but they could not even protect their own backyard. Sherif Hussein was sent packing by Ibn Saud in 1925 as his former subjects eagerly celebrated not their conquest but their liberation. By then, Churchill, at Lawrence and Bell's urging, had created the kingdom of Iraq just for Hussein's son Faisal. It did not prove to be a happy or wise decision. Meanwhile, the real power in Arabia was Ibn Saud's.

The founding father

Ibn Saud built the Kingdom of Saudi Arabia and unified its tribes through the imposition of puritanical Wahhabi Islam as a reaction to the allegedly cosmopolitan, corrupt, and decaying Ottoman caliphate in Constantinople. But it is a wild distortion to argue that traditional Saudi Wahhabism is equivalent to the Islamic radicalism that swept the Muslim world in the 1980s. The source of that later radicalism was Ayatollah Ruhullah Khomeini's Islamic Revolution in Iran. Both Ibn Saud's Wahhabist revolt and Khomeini's Shiite revolt can be seen as the equivalent of the Protestant Reformation, but the latter was far more radical than the former.

Ibn Saud sat out both world wars but never showed the partiality for the Nazis that other Arab leaders (like Haj Amin al-Husseini, the commanders of the British-trained Iraqi army, and even Anwar Sadat) notoriously did. And he was implacable in his hatred of Communism as a diabolical revolutionary force. He felt the same way about Zionism, for that matter. But he was also throughout his life a great and appreciative friend of the United States. He loathed Jews, but he was appalled and disgusted by the Holocaust.

Ibn Saud built his kingdom not by destroying old values and ways but by restoring and cherishing them. He was the exemplar of a classic Bedouin sheikh. Many of the (true) stories told about him would fit characters like Jethro and Abraham in the Bible, or the first generation of Arab leaders after Muhammad. Unlike Gamal Abdel Nasser in Egypt, Ibn Saud never tried to destabilize or subvert neighboring nations. Western styles of parliamentary democracy were alien and ludicrous to him, but he carefully practiced the traditional desert Arab forms of mediation and consultation within his tribe and society. It is because his sons all have continued that practice over the five and a half decades since his death that Saudi Arabia, against so many predictions of doom to the contrary, has remained as stable and successful as it has.

King Faisal and the oil weapon

Faisal ibn Abdulaziz became king of Saudi Arabia in 1964. His ascent to the throne had not been ensured—except by his talent. He was one of Ibn Saud's older sons, but not the heir apparent in the line of succession. But it was clear long before the death of his father in 1952 that he was the old man's favorite. At Lake Success in 1947, the young Prince Faisal had led the Arab nations' fierce opposition to the UN's partition plan to create the State of Israel. Of all the desert kingdom's rulers over the next sixty years, he would prove by far the most implacable in his opposition to the very existence of the Jewish state.

But when Faisal came to power, Saudi Arabia appeared to be in trouble. His useless brother King Saud ibn Abdulaziz had squandered the kingdom's growing oil revenues while letting the consortium of U.S. oil companies in Aramco enjoy a free hand. Saudi Arabia appeared under threat from revolutionary Communist and Arab socialist subversion. The charismatic Gamal Abdel Nasser was riding high across the entire region after defying the British and the French in 1956.

Conservative monarchies seemed to be toppling across the Middle East. Revolutionary regimes that wanted to overthrow the Saudi monarchy now existed on the country's northern and eastern borders. The Iraqi monarchy had been mercilessly massacred by a military coup in 1958. Nasser was making Egypt the region's military mini-superpower with Soviet weapons, and Syria was its ally. Faisal, devoutly Muslim and passionately loyal to the desert traditions of his Bedouin people and to the memory of his late father, seemed a ridiculous anachronism in the modern Arab world. Instead, he was about to transform it in his image.

Characters like Faisal's ousted brother King Saud, the obese playboy King Farouk of Egypt, and King Faisal I of Iraq, the darling of T. E. Lawrence, Churchill, and Gertrude Bell, had led many Westerners and Communists to assume all hereditary Arab monarchs could be written off as weak and decadent. But the religiously devout Faisal was not. He was a quiet, methodical, and even shy workaholic who set about cleaning up the wrecked finances of his country and studying the terms of its relationship with the American oil companies. He was not given to

Un-PC History: Great Men Change the World

"It is not fashionable today to construct history around heroes. The anthropology, sociology, and economics of Arabia in the early years of this century should, in theory, explain how the disparate sheikhdoms, towns, and tribes of the peninsula came together to form this massive and extraordinary state. But they do not. The only satisfactory answer resides in the unique vision and skills of Abdulaziz himself."

Ronald Lacey, *The Kingdom: Arabia and the House of Saud*

grandiose, empty speeches like Nasser. He hated Communism with at least as much passion as he did Zionism. He proved a formidable enemy to both.

Faisal realized that the Hashemite line no longer posed any threat to oil-rich Saudi Arabia. The Hashemite royal house had been extinguished in Iraq, and King Hussein's Jordan was too small to worry about. Indeed, Faisal realized the advantage of keeping Jordan in King Hussein's cautious and responsible hands. That way Faisal could support Yasser Arafat and his young PLO against Israel, but also use Jordan as a buffer, preventing it from being another revolutionary bridgehead like Iraq, Syria, and Egypt.

Faisal was helped by world events. In 1967—the same epochal year that Israel smashed Nasser's dreams and conquered the West Bank, Gaza, and the holy city of Jerusalem—the great oil reserves of Texas started to fall short. Faisal benefited from his vast experience as a diplomat serving his late father and as the most respected senior figure in the kingdom during the reign of his worthless brother. In return for richly funding the PLO in its guerrilla attacks against Israel and Israeli and Jewish targets around the world, he won immunity for his country from PLO troublemaking and subversion that afflicted Jordan and Lebanon. He authorized his oil ministers to start negotiating with Shah Reza Pahlavi, the autocratic dictator of Shiite Iran across the Persian Gulf, about coordinating their policies on fixing oil prices.

After the death of Nasser in 1970, Faisal found his successor, Anwar Sadat, a welcome change. Sadat did not have Nasser's grandiose ambitions to wreak revolution and havoc throughout the Arab world. Like Faisal, he was ready to work cooperatively with the Americans and was anti-Soviet. And he offered the only realistic Arab military option against Israel. The two men created a new Saudi-Egyptian axis that remains a key factor for stability in the Arab world today.

In 1973, when Sadat threw 80,000 Egyptian soldiers against Israel's hollow shell of a defensive line on the east side of the Suez Canal, Faisal struck too. Over the following weeks, to the shock and then horror of the world, Saudi Arabia and Iran led Iraq, Indonesia, Venezuela, and the other main oil-

Sound Monarchies

"The important thing about a regime is not what it is called but how it acts. There are corrupt republican regimes and sound monarchies, and vice versa....The quality of a regime should be judged by its deeds and the integrity of its rulers."

King Faisal ibn Abdulaziz, quoted in Ronald Lacey, *The Kingdom: Arabia and the House of Saud*

producing nations in arbitrarily raising the price of oil. In a few months, they had quadrupled it.

Britain and France had fully withdrawn from the Middle East. The United States was exhausted and demoralized from the war in Vietnam. None of the major Western powers had either the military clout or the nerve to try to move against the key oil-producing nations, either by invasion or by fomenting a coup. Besides, Saudi Arabia and Iran were—supposedly—the United States' main allies in the region. Nixon and Henry Kissinger had eagerly built up the shah of Iran as their regional policeman to keep the Soviets and Arab revolutionary regimes out of the Saudi and Kuwaiti oil fields. The Saudis, however, had rightly judged that the shah was an unstable and unpredictable megalomaniac whom the Americans could not trust, and Faisal offered the shah a deal he couldn't refuse: vastly increased oil revenues. The "oil weapon" was born.

Faisal did not hesitate to use it on a global scale. Threatened with the big stick of soaring oil prices, or having crucial oil supplies withheld, dozens of nations ended their diplomatic relations with Israel. Third World countries expelled Israeli development teams who were part of Prime Minister Golda Meir's fatuous attempt to make Israel the leader of a new Third World power bloc. As the African nations fell obediently in line behind the Saudis, the United Nations was transformed overnight into a relentless global megaphone of rejection and hate against Israel and the United States. Faisal made no secret of his dark side. He was not just implacably anti-Zionist and devoted to the annihilation of Israel, but equally anti-Semitic. He believed the ancient, long-discredited "blood libel" that Jews killed Muslim and Christian children and used their blood to bake Passover matzos. He believed *The Protocols of the Elders of Zion*, the forged Jewish plot to conquer the world concocted by the Okhrana, the czarist Russian secret police. Hitler had used the *Protocols* as one of his justifications for the Holocaust, and historian Norman Cohn rightly called it a "warrant for genocide." Faisal enthusiastically gave copies of it to his visitors as gifts.

Faisal was, as it turned out, far ahead of his time in championing a revived pan-Arab movement based on religious extremism. He dramatically stepped up funding of *madrassas*, Islamic religious schools, across the Islamic world. He was not typical of his successors, but he set Saudi policy along fateful paths that his successors did not dare to change.

There is no telling how much further Faisal might have gone. Would he have made common cause with Ronald Reagan to bring the Soviet Union down, as his successors did? He might have—or he might have refused because of Reagan's strong support for Israel. He might well have made common cause instead with Ayatollah Khomeini after the Islamic Revolution in Iran. The prospect of Saudi Arabia and Iran united in implacable opposition to the United States and Israel could have transformed the world in the early 1980s, and not for the better.

But on March 25, 1975, at a *majlis*, a traditional gathering of Saudi royals, where even the most obscure and junior members were granted access and allowed to present their grievances and concerns, King Faisal was shot dead. He fell victim not to a Communist, Nasserite, or extreme Islamist revolutionary, but to his own nephew, a mentally deranged drug addict who had hung out in California. The killer was convicted of regicide and beheaded three months later.

Saudi Arabia's three threats

King Faisal was followed by King Khaled (1975–1982), King Fahd (1982–2005), and King Abdullah (acting as crown prince and regent, 1995–2005). During these years, Saudi Arabia regarded the three greatest threats to its existence as a revolutionary Iran, an aggressive or unstable Iraq, and Islamic radicalism.

Saudi attitudes toward Iran had fluctuated wildly since the 1979 Islamic Revolution, finally culminating in fear of the radical Shiites, which pushed the kingdom into the arms of Ronald Reagan. Like the United States, the Saudis under King Fahd financed Saddam Hussein in his war against Iran until 1988. When, however, Saddam swallowed Kuwait in July 1990, the terrified Saudi leaders realized they could very easily be next. Relations with the United States became even closer, and Saudi Arabia became the marshalling yard for the U.S-led 700,000 strong allied army—the greatest ever gathered in the Middle East—that smashed Saddam's military power in the 1991 Gulf War.

Relations with the United States slowly deteriorated during the Clinton years, however. It didn't help when cautious and tactful Warren Christopher was replaced as secretary of state in Clinton's second term by in-your-face, pro-democracy Madeleine Albright. Also, King Fahd was slowly dying, and by the late 1990s, effective power in the kingdom had passed to his brother Crown Prince Abdullah ibn Abdulaziz. While cautiously pro-American, Abdullah was much more traditional and incorruptible than Fahd. He lost confidence in Clinton and Albright and was concerned about the financial effect of plummeting global oil prices on the kingdom's fiscal stability. He also noted that Iran had elected its most moderate leader since before

Saudi Arabia vs. the Terrorists

"Al Qaeda underestimated the efficacy of Saudi intelligence and security forces and their ability to adapt to new types of threat and attack. While ordinary police were not equipped to deal with the new threat, Saudi intelligence was able to accurately identify those militants who comprised the twenty-six most-wanted list as leaders of al Qaeda relatively quickly, and the security services were able to hunt down and disrupt most of the cells they headed."

Anthony Cordesman and Nawaf Obaid, of Washington's Center for Strategic and International Studies, "Al Qaeda in Saudi Arabia: Asymmetric Threats and Islamist Extremists," 2005

the 1979 revolution, Mohammad Khatami. So in 1999 Saudi Abdullah concluded an oil production limiting and price-control agreement with Iran. The two giants quickly showed they still had the clout within OPEC,

Harry St. John Philby: The Anti-Lawrence

T. E. Lawrence was a romantic dreamer who acted out his crazed fantasies. But the unsung giant of the Middle East of Lawrence's time was Harry "Jack" Philby. Philby was another Englishman gone native, but unlike Lawrence, who embraced the unpopular and ineffectual Hashemite family, he befriended Abdulaziz ibn Saud and became the highly influential advisor to the real power in the Arabian desert. In the early 1930s, to his vast personal gain, he helped negotiate between Ibn Saud and Standard Oil of California, granting the company the prospecting concession for oil in the eastern part of the kingdom. Philby turned his back on England and converted to Islam (and accepted its requirement of circumcision) in middle age. His son Kim, who worked for the British secret service, became even more infamous than his father, serving as a spy for the Soviet Union for a quarter-century until he defected there in 1963.

If nothing else, Jack Philby was a realist. He did not try to impose his own vision on the Middle East but clearly recognized its winners and losers and the crucial importance of oil. He served his master Ibn Saud loyally and well, and in the process, served the national interests of the United States superbly. He died a wealthy man, in his own bed, at a ripe old age.

As Ronald Lacey notes in his book *The Kingdom: Arabia and the House of Saud*, "There was much that was noble, little that was gracious, about Harry St. John Philby. That was probably why he got on so well with the Arabs."

given the right circumstances, to make a difference. Over the next four years, oil prices trebled from around ten dollars a barrel to more than thirty. It seemed like a lot of money at the time.

President Khatami served two terms in power, but his successor in 2005 was a very different kind of man. King Abdullah met with President Mahmoud Ahmadinejad and, according to Saudi sources, quickly became alarmed at how irrational and unpredictable he could be. It was a good argument for stabilizing relations with the United States.

Unfortunately for the Saudis, from their point of view, the United States wasn't acting cautiously or responsibly in the Middle East either, after the 2003 Iraq War and the ousting of Saddam Hussein. They were privately happy to see Saddam gone, but they knew from firsthand experience that Western liberal democracy doesn't work in their part of the world.

The Saudis were also very wary of Iraq's Sunni-Shiite feud spilling into their own country. Popular opinion among Sunni Muslims in Saudi Arabia was strongly engaged on the side of the Sunnis in Iraq. But oil-rich Dhahran is home to many Shiites, perhaps even a majority. The Saudis responded by building a massive, costly security barrier on their northern border.

The Saudis had an even more immediate concern. By 2006, the U.S. military was noting an increasing number of young Saudis active in the Sunni insurgency in Iraq, particularly in the ranks of the suicide bombers. This identification was predictable, but it frightened the Saudis. Saudi support for the anti-Communist mujahedin in Afghanistan had produced bin Laden, al Qaeda, September 11, and the 2003 bombings in Saudi Arabia. The Iraq civil war threatened to produce a far larger number of radicalized Saudis committed to toppling their own government. So the Saudis cracked down on the radical religious teachers within their own borders. While trying to seal their northern borders, they also tried to seal their southern border with Yemen, whence an estimated 400,000 people a year were trekking north for a better life. The Saudis, suspecting radical elements in impoverished Yemen were infiltrating their kingdom, acted to shut them down by building another security fence.

The Saudi monarchy will always have its own national interests, but the interests of a conservative monarchy are much more likely to align in the future, as they have in the past, with America's desire for a stable, non-Communist, non-radical Middle East. And if we will take the Saudis' advice, conservative, tradition-minded monarchies are a better bet for the future of a pro-Western Middle East than are Islamic democracies and the Islamists they might elect.

Chapter 8

MIDDLE EAST WARS AND PEACE
1975–2007

It's popular to assert that the Middle East has always been a blood-bath, but it's not true. Indeed, when the 1973 Yom Kippur War ended, a period of peace set in (interrupted, of course, with bouts of violence). It lasted nearly thirty years.

Israel's relations with its neighboring Arab states were dominated by dynamics of peace, not war. Anwar Sadat made peace with Israel in the 1977–1979 period. A strange state of theoretical war that was really peace operated on the Golan Heights between Israel and Syria. Lebanon collapsed into a horrendous civil war largely instigated by Yasser Arafat and his PLO, and first Syria and then Israel let themselves get sucked into the infernal brew, with Syria getting by far the better of it. Saudi Arabia, Jordan, Egypt, and the Arab Gulf states all enjoyed peace, and all of them except Egypt prospered. Even in Egypt, there were welcome decades of peace and development in striking contrast to the heroic but hysterical and ruinous adventures of Nasser's era.

Arabs can fight

Americans and Israelis in particular in the decades since the dramatic Israeli victories in the 1967 Six-Day War have widely embraced the myth that Arabs can't win wars. This attitude appears to have been shared by

Guess what?

- The Ba'ath Party was founded by Western-educated elitists as a party of social justice and socialist reformation.

- Syrian president Hafez Assad hated Israel but respected Yitzhak Rabin, and he loved Palestine but hated Yasser Arafat.

- The American president with the best Middle East record? Not Carter, not Clinton, but Gerald Ford.

Vice President Dick Cheney, Defense Secretary Donald Rumsfeld, and their handpicked advisors when they sent the U.S. armed forces sweeping into Iraq in March 2003 and thought they could redraw the political map of the country at will.

In fact, the military history of the twentieth century shows that not only can Arabs fight, but they can do so very well.

The Arab Middle East was one of the last areas of the world to resist conquest and colonization by the great European powers. Britain and France got their hands on it only when the Ottoman Empire finally collapsed after a long, tough, bitter fight in late 1918. It should be noted that most of the soldiers who surrounded, trapped, and ultimately captured the Anglo-Indian army at Kut in 1915 were Arabs recruited by the Ottomans from within the region. And they were among the very first to drive out the British and French. By 1948 every major Arab nation except Algeria was independent, and by 1958 every one of them had successfully ejected all British and French influence over their affairs. This was not the record of nations of cowards, incompetents, or defeatists.

It is true that Israel has won all the major conventional military wars against its Arab neighbors, often against formidable odds. But the Israelis were almost always fighting for their survival. Mass conscript Arab armies were sent into wars far from home, like the luckless Egyptian armies Nasser sent into Yemen in the 1960s and those destroyed by the Israelis in 1948, 1956, and 1967.

But the performance of the Iraqi army against vastly numerically superior Iranian forces during the eight-year Iran-Iraq War was excellent. The Iraqis had brave and excellent field commanders—until Saddam Hussein, murderous and witless as ever, killed the best of them himself—and ordinary Iraqi soldiers fought long and bravely with great discipline. Most important of all, they won.

In conventional wars, whenever Arab soldiers have been equipped, trained, and armed to fight modern Western armies on anything like equal terms, especially in defense of their homeland, they have usually fought bravely and well. The Israeli troops who fought the Jordanian and Syrian armies in 1967 and the Syrians and Egyptians in 1973 have testified to the toughness of their opponents.

It was true that U.S. forces quickly annihilated the Iraqi conventional forces in the 1991 and 2003 Gulf Wars. But that wasn't because they were fighting Arabs. It was because weak, underdeveloped nations usually can't stand up to major industrial states, let alone superpowers, in quick, straightforward campaigns.

But when it came to guerrilla war, Muslim Arab nations proved to be some of the toughest foes in the world in the second half of the twentieth century. The National Liberation Front of Algeria proved far more ferocious and ruthless than even the Vietnamese in their eight-year war of independence against France from 1954 to 1962. The Israelis have yet to destroy Hezbollah, whose forces eventually drove them out of southern Lebanon. The mujahedin guerrillas in Afghanistan eventually drove out the Soviets after another eight-year war. And the Sunni Muslim guerrillas in central Iraq, at the present time, have yet to be operationally defeated or destroyed by U.S. and coalition forces.

That is a pretty impressive record by anybody's standards. Over the past sixty years, the nations of Continental Europe, Latin America, and sub-Saharan Africa cannot begin to compete with it.

The Ba'ath Party's socialist roots

Even opponents of the Iraq War admit that Saddam Hussein was a brutal dictator, and his Ba'ath Party was a totalitarian oppressor. What you won't find the Left admitting is this: Ba'athism has its source in the idealistic pipe dreams of elite, educated Marxists.

Throughout the past four decades, Syria and Iraq, the two great Arab nations of the Fertile Crescent, have been ruled by the Ba'ath Resurrection

(Arab Socialist Party). Ba'ath rule brought endless economic stagnation, wars of foreign aggression, support for murderous terrorist organizations, apparently endless dictatorships, secret police tyrannies, massacres of tens of thousands of civilians in rebellious populations, and thousands of hair-raising examples of sadistic torture in underground dungeons.

Yet the Ba'ath Party was founded by misty-eyed, romantic revolutionaries (one might even call them innocents) who foresaw nothing but a bright golden age of peace, prosperity, and understanding for the Arab world under their enlightened rule. Provided no one got in the way, of course. It was the story of the Young Turks and their Committee of Union and Progress all over again. Like the Young Turks, the idealists of the Ba'ath Party proved the wisdom of British political philosopher Sir Isaiah Berlin: every attempt to create a perfect utopia on earth is guaranteed to create hell on earth instead.

Two Damascus schoolteachers—Michel Aflaq, a Christian, and Salah ad-Din al-Bitar, a Muslim—co-founded the Ba'ath Party in 1940. They wanted to end hatred and distrust between Christians and Muslims. They wanted to create a single, unified Arab nation across the Middle East founded on peace and social justice. They wanted to abolish poverty. They were all in favor of freedom and democracy and, of course, all for socialism. They hated tyranny in every form—or thought they did.

But far from uniting the Arab world, the Ba'ath movement shattered it. Far from establishing freedom and democracy, it established the longest-lasting, most stable, and bloody tyrannies in modern Arab history. The contrast with King Abdullah and King Hussein in Jordan, or with King Abdulaziz and his successors in Saudi Arabia, could not be greater. Far from joining together, the two nations where Ba'ath parties took and held power—Syria and Iraq—were the most bitter rivals and enemies for generations, each of them claiming to be the only heir and embodiment of true Ba'athism while the other was evil heresy. In the year 1984, two versions of Big Brother that George Orwell would have recognized only too well were alive and ruling in Damascus and Baghdad. They would stay there for decades to come.

Arab tyrants: Assad and Saddam

After its humiliating defeat at Israel's hands in the 1947–1948 war, through 1970, Syria changed governments faster than a revolving door swings. There were at least twenty-five different governments in twenty-two years. The Syrian republic became a laughingstock throughout the Middle East, and its armed forces were a byword for passive incompetence. The Syrian army played no role whatsoever in the 1956 Israeli-Egyptian Sinai war. In 1967, after their air force was destroyed on the ground in the first hours of the war, they sat passively until Israeli defense minister Moshe Dayan was able to amass overwhelming forces to take the Golan Heights from them.

But in the thirty-eight years since 1970, the Syrian government has not fallen once. The only change in its leadership came in 2000, when tough old President Hafez Assad died in his bed at the age of sixty-nine after thirty years of uncontested supreme power. His surviving son Bashar took over immediately as president and not a whisper of dissent was heard against it.

Assad also left behind as his lasting legacy the toughest military force in the Arab world, one that had faced the Israeli army in full land combat more often and performed more effectively against it than any other. Assad's achievement contrasts not only with Syria's past, but also with the fate of his fellow and rival Ba'ath dictator, President Saddam Hussein, in neighboring Iraq.

Both men came to power at almost the same time. Assad seized power in Damascus in 1970, determined to erase the humiliation and shame his nation, its armed forces, and most of all his air force had suffered at Israel's hands in the 1967 Six-Day War. In 1968 Saddam became the number-two man and real power behind the throne in the Second Ba'ath Republic led by President Ahmed Hassan al-Bakr.

Assad and Saddam were both merciless tyrants who routinely employed torture on an unprecedented scale. Both of them waged wars of aggression and conquest against their neighbors. And neither of them hesitated to slaughter many thousands of their own citizens whenever they felt it necessary or expedient to do so. Both of them looked to the Soviet Union for weapons and support, and both of them hated the state of Israel like poison.

Ironically, through the 1980s, it was Saddam who was seen in American eyes (especially those of Reagan administration policymakers) as by far the more moderate of the two. Saddam was battling the Shiite Islamic fanatics of Ayatollah Khomeini's Iran from sweeping across the Middle East. Assad, by contrast, was forging a long-term alliance between Syria and Iran. American policymakers saw Syria, not Iraq, as directing and protecting the most dangerous terrorist forces in the region through the 1980s. In 1983, Shiite Hezbollah suicide bombers backed by both Iran and Syria killed more than 250 U.S. Marines and more than 60 French paratroopers as they slept in their barracks on the outskirts of Beirut.

But it was Assad who died in his bed, with his son surviving to rule as his heir and his regime and formidable army securely in place. Saddam, who had inherited a far larger and more populous nation with the second-largest oil reserves on earth and a far larger and more

Good Intentions

"We thought that the epochs of darkness had come to an end with our predecessors among the politicians and that we were the glorious beginning of a new civilization, when we were in fact the last exemplars of backwardness, and a desolating expression of it."

Sami al-Jundi, *The Ba'ath*

powerful army—the fourth largest in the world by 1990—squandered all of those assets before dying on December 30, 2006, at the end of a hangman's rope.

Assad's lasting success remains ignored or underrated by U.S. and Israeli policymakers to this day. But there are sobering lessons to be learned from why he succeeded where Saddam and Nasser did not.

The fearsome Sphinx of Damascus was a study in contrasts. He commanded the Syrian air force in the worst defeat in its history, yet used that defeat as a springboard to power. He inherited an army regarded as a bad joke throughout its own region and within three years made it formidable. It remains so to this day.

Assad led an Arab nationalist regime, yet he slaughtered Islamic believers and fundamentalists more ruthlessly and on a far wider scale than Saddam ever dared to. He held power for thirty years through the use of torture and terror and he came from a tiny ethnic and religious sect traditionally distrusted by his nation's overwhelmingly Sunni Muslim majority. Yet he appears to have enjoyed real support and respect, and his son has ruled relatively securely since his death.

Assad was the most dangerous enemy the State of Israel had after the death of Gamal Abdel Nasser. Yet he forged a lasting bond of respect with one of Israel's greatest leaders: Yitzhak Rabin, whom he never met in person. He championed the Palestinian cause passionately, but he hated and despised the man who was the living embodiment of that cause: Yasser Arafat.

The first secret of Hafez Assad's success was that he ruled according to Niccolo Machiavelli, not James Madison. He would have regarded the second Bush administration's obsession with creating instant full-scale Western representative democracy and freedom throughout the Middle East not only as threatening his own power, but as a contemptible joke for ignoring the power realities of the region, its history, and political and military realities.

In the late 1990s, future Bush administration policymakers and intellectuals, led by David Wurmser, Vice President Dick Cheney's chief Middle East advisor, openly described nations like Iraq and Syria as "failed states," ignoring the fact that they had been around as distinct national entities since the early 1920s. And Saddam in Iraq and Assad in Syria both solved the problems of chronic instability that had plagued both nations for the twenty years before either of them took power.

Assad, heeding Machiavelli's counsel, regarded being feared as vastly more important than being loved. But though he killed widely, he did not, as Saddam did, kill continually or indiscriminately. In Iraq the wives and even children of those who crossed Saddam, even by contradicting him or one of his murderous sons in a conversation, were tortured, raped, mutilated, and murdered. Assad did those things only to his enemies, although there were enough of them.

In 1982, Assad crushed a popular uprising on behalf of the Islamist Muslim Brotherhood in the western Syrian city of Hama by annihilating the entire city. Tanks and heavy artillery were sent in to pulverize the remains. When U.S. intelligence analysts compared before and after photographs of the city from surveillance satellites they could not believe their own eyes. The death toll of civilians is generally estimated at 20,000, and it may even have been much higher. Rifaat Assad, Hafez's brother and longtime secret police chief, later claimed to U.S. journalist Thomas Friedman that the death toll was really 38,000. Not even Saddam ever authorized killing against his own people with such intensity.

But where Saddam killed endlessly, and appears to have had a psychotic need to do it, Assad killed only when it clearly served his interests. The domestic nature of the two regimes was very different. Saddam ran a grim, utterly totalitarian state that survivors of Josef Stalin's 1930s terror would have recognized all too well. Every public utterance on anything had to be in total conformity with the decrees of the Great National Leader, otherwise the torture chamber, the firing squad, or the hangman beckoned. In Syria, by contrast, those who stayed out of politics and public discourse could expect to live their own lives and even modestly enjoy their own private property.

The foreign policies and patterns of aggression of the two regimes were very different. Assad craved to control Lebanon, as more ineffectual Syrian rulers before him had, just as Saddam was determined to reincorporate Kuwait as the nineteenth province of Iraq, as Iraqi nationalists before him had.

Both of them did it, but Saddam openly and brutally invaded Kuwait in July 1990 and brought the entire military might of the United States and its allies down on his head only six months later. Assad craftily encouraged dissent, civil war, and chaos in Lebanon before sending in his army—supposedly to restore order—in 1976. He was able to stay there for six years until the Israelis drove him out.

Saddam was mercilessly invincible in Iraq for thirty-five years from the establishment of the second Ba'ath Republic in 1968, where he held the real power for eleven years before ousting the ineffectual figurehead al-Bakr. (He had Bakr murdered by being pumped full of insulin three years later.)

But Saddam knew nothing about the world outside Iraq, and he miscalculated catastrophically every time he provoked it. Assad never did. He retained the strong support of the Soviet Union and later Russia from beginning to end. The Sphinx of Damascus defied the United States and undermined its influence successfully for decades, then came to a kind of accommodation with Washington during the Clinton administration when he had to. He even hosted two U.S. presidents on visits: Richard Nixon and Bill Clinton.

Assad's relations with Israel were extraordinary in their achievements and complexity. Within three years of taking power, he unleashed the Syrian army to take the Jewish state by surprise in the first hours of the 1973 Yom Kippur War.

The Israelis eventually turned the tide against overwhelming forces in the Golan fighting against Syria and drove back to within artillery range of Damascus when a cease-fire was finally imposed. But although the Israelis could probably have taken the Syrian capital and could certainly have leveled it had the war continued, they never succeeded in routing the Syrians or in surrounding them, as Ariel Sharon was able to do against the Egyptian Third Army on the west bank of the Suez Canal.

As guerrilla attacks, especially from Hezbollah, grew in 1982 after the Israeli military conquest of southern Lebanon, Assad was able to win back through guerrilla war and diplomatic skill what he had lost in direct war. By 1984 Israel was forced out of most of southern Lebanon except for a buffer region north of its border. Some sixteen years later, Israeli prime minister Ehud Barak pulled out of there too. Hezbollah was able to establish a state within a state in the southern part of the country, and Syrian military forces and intelligence organizations moved back in to dominate much of the country for almost the next quarter-century. Saddam, by contrast, had been unable to hang on to Kuwait for more than six months.

But even while he was supporting tough, ruthless, and firmly effective guerrilla forces fighting the Israelis as Syrian (and Iranian) proxies in southern Lebanon, Assad ran no risks with provoking them on the Golan Heights, where troops of both nations continued to face each other. In the twenty-five years from the signing of the Israeli-Syrian disengagement agreement in 1975 to Assad's death in 2000, not a single Israeli or Syrian soldier died in any incident on the Golan front. The long peace lasted through the first seven years after his death, though there are now many indications it may not last for much longer.

Ford's Middle East successes

If you believe your PC history books, there have been only three kind of Republican presidents since Lincoln: evil ones (Nixon and Hoover), dumb ones (Reagan and Coolidge), and Teddy Roosevelt. For the media at the time and mainstream historians these days, there was no choice but to stick Gerald Ford into the dunce category.

He was supposed to be a brainless, muddling, old football player and political hack who had received one blow to the head too many. Gerald Ford ranks with his fellow moderate Republican Warren G. Harding as the most underestimated American president of the twentieth century. And his Middle East record was possibly the best of any president.

Dwight Eisenhower "lost" Egypt to the Russians, and Ford, by his approval of Henry Kissinger's most complicated, subtle, patient, and successful diplomatic maneuvers, brought it back into the American orbit as never before. He also guided the American economy through the worst aspects of the 1973–1974 quadrupling of global oil prices and stabilized the economy with some of the strongest, most courageous, and most unpopular leadership it had seen in decades.

On both the home and foreign affairs fronts, the quiet, hardworking Ford provided decisive, successful leadership that was increasingly respected around the world. Only the American people, led by liberal pundits foaming at the mouth over Ford's pardon for Nixon to end the long national nightmare of the Watergate scandal, couldn't see it.

Kissinger, curiously, did far better running around the region as Ford's secretary of state than he had as Nixon's right-hand man. It might have been that Nixon kept Kissinger on a much tighter leash than anyone realized while Ford loosened the reins. It might also have been that the almost cataclysmic consequences of the Yom Kippur War—the threatened destruction of Israel and the risk of a thermonuclear showdown between the United States and the Soviet Union—followed by the OPEC embargo had concentrated U.S. policymakers' focus on the region. For the first time, Kissinger was not dealing primarily with the Soviet Union, China, Pakistan, Iran, or the Vietnam War. The Middle East was the biggest issue on his agenda. In any case, with Ford backing him to the hilt, he did very well.

First, Kissinger engaged in months of endless negotiations, charming, lies, flattery, bribery, and threats with Israel and Egypt to bring about the 1975 Sinai II Disengagement Agreement. This proved to be one of the most successful, far-reaching, and overlooked diplomatic achievements in modern American history. It ended the apparently inevitable and endless cycle of wars between Israel and Egypt—five wars in twenty-five years to that point. It gave Israel a vital breathing space for recovery after its heavy casualties of the 1973 war but without paying anything like the price Israeli prime minister Menachem Begin had to pay for a full peace treaty with Egypt. Prime Minister Yitzhak Rabin won the far-reaching Matmon C arms package from the United States that forever changed the essential construction of the Israeli army. In paving the way for Matmon C, the disengagement agreement also laid the basis for the next thirty years of unquestioned Israeli security and military predominance in the region.

Sinai II also prepared the way for Kissinger's triumph of negotiating a similar armistice agreement between Israel and Syria, which proved just as successful and long-lasting. It even paved the way for an unlikely Israeli-Syrian strategic understanding that lasted for twenty-five years.

Finally, Ford grasped the opportunity with Anwar Sadat that Nixon had ignored after the expulsion of the Soviet diplomats in 1971: he started a long-lasting U.S. strategic relationship with Egypt. Sadat quickly knew the United States could give him far more than the Soviets had ever provided. And unlike Nasser, Sadat also realized that Soviet economic wisdom was the fast road to even worse poverty and destitution. U.S. economic aid and Western tourism were set to flood in to keep Egypt stable and afloat for at least another three decades. Given the huge rate of population increase during the same time, it was impossible to hope for, let alone achieve, anything more.

Skillful and successful in their dealings with Egypt and Syria, Ford and Kissinger were also lucky in their experiences with Saudi Arabia. In 1975, King Faisal, the most successful and formidable ruler since old Ibn

Saud himself, was assassinated by a mentally disturbed nephew. His successor and half-brother, King Khaled, was a different kind of man—decent, cautious, and low-key. He in turn bequeathed effective power to his own heir and half brother, Crown Prince Fahd. And Fahd, while brilliant and forceful like Faisal, was profoundly pro-American. His takeover of effective power in Riyadh eased relations with the United States, took military confrontation with Israel off the front burner, and prepared the way for the strategic partnership between Saudi Arabia and the United States under Ronald Reagan that would play such a huge role in bringing down the Soviet Union.

Oil prices remained high, times in the United States remained relatively tough, and Khaled and Fahd were not disposed to reduce the oil prices and cut off the financial bonanza Faisal had provided for them. For that matter, neither did the shah of Iran. But when Gerald Ford left office in January 1977—quietly, gracefully, with good humor and head held high, the way no American president had left the Oval Office since Dwight Eisenhower's departure in 1961—he left behind a stabilized Middle East, full of opportunity and hope for his successor. Jimmy Carter would reap the rewards of the good seeds Ford had sowed, but he also wrecked nearly all of it.

Kissinger's realpolitik

The key to Ford's success, admittedly, was Henry Kissinger. A German Jew whose family fled the Nazis in World War II, Kissinger was a brilliant Harvard professor of diplomatic history with a remarkable gift for political intrigue. So skillful was he that during the 1968 presidential campaign he was a front-runner to become national security advisor with both main candidates at the same time—Republican Richard M. Nixon and Democrat Hubert H. Humphrey. When Nixon edged out Humphrey in a squeaker election, Kissinger got the job. In 1973, he rose still higher to serve as secretary of state under Nixon and then under Ford.

Kissinger specialized in *realpolitik* policies that accomplished moral goals while appearing utterly cynical and confounding apparent common sense. Before he entered the Middle East arena, it was universally assumed that you had to back one side or the other in the Israeli-Arab conflict, and if the United States backed Israel, it would continue to steadily lose power and influence across the Arab world.

The Effective Barbarian

Mustafa Tlass was Syria's minister of defense for thirty-two years (from 1972 to 2004). So it is safe to say that his stamp is on the country. What does that mean? Well, Tlass publicly boasted about torturing and castrating Israeli prisoners after the 1973 Yom Kippur War. In the 1980s he wrote and published a book proclaiming the truth of the ancient anti-Semitic blood libel that Jews kill Christian and Muslim children and use their blood to bake Passover matzos. He reportedly kept a large pin-up of the famous Italian movie actress Gina Lollobrigida in his office for many years. Because of his love for her, he said, he made sure the Italian peacekeeping force was spared from the devastating 1983 suicide truck bomb attacks that killed more than three hundred American and French soldiers in Lebanon.

It would be easy to caricature Tlass as a barbaric savage or a buffoon. But he was the most powerful Sunni Muslim in the regime of President Hafez Assad, and he loyally helped assure the success of Assad's son Bashar. He also made Syria a far more formidable military power in the Middle East (modeling his force on Soviet armored doctrine). In any future wars, Syria will certainly not fight by Marquis of Queensberry or Geneva Convention rules, thanks to Tlass.

Kissinger confounded this assumption. By maintaining and strengthening the U.S. role as Israel's chief supporter, he made Washington the place Arab leaders had to go if they wanted any concessions from the Israelis. As Israel was dependent only on the United States, it followed that only the United States could bring pressure to bear. It all seemed so obvious once you started to think about it.

Kissinger went on to displace and replace Soviet influence in Egypt with American. He also brought relative peace and stability to the region by selling arms to both sides in the Israel-Arab conflict. This was good news for major U.S. companies hurting from the quadrupling of oil prices in the 1970s. It also dramatically revived long-lasting U.S. influence in the region.

Kissinger and Nixon were by no means infallible when it came to dealing with the Middle East. They came up with the Nixon Doctrine to maintain security in the oil-rich Persian Gulf by building up the shah of Iran as a regional military power comparable to Israel. But the shah proved to be first an ungrateful and backstabbing ally, and then a giant with feet of clay. He played a crucial leading role in the cartel with Saudi Arabia and other Arab nations in quadrupling global oil prices. Within another five years, he was gone entirely, toppled by a furious old Shiite Muslim cleric he had banished to Paris.

Kissinger also miscalculated in delaying crucial aid to Israel during the 1973 Yom Kippur War. He wanted Israel to survive the war but to be chastened by it, so its leaders would be more willing to compromise with the major Arab states on his terms. But the war moved so fast that the Israeli army risked running out of ammunition and weapons against the Egyptians. Desperate Israeli appeals to President Nixon finally convinced Kissinger to resupply. But Defense Secretary James Schlesinger played the key role in pushing through the organization of the famous C-5A Galaxy airlift that got the crucial supplies to the Israeli troops in time.

Still, Kissinger's subtle, cynical, micromanaged, hyperactive, and self-glorifying diplomacy worked, launching the first real peace process between Israel and its Arab neighbors and enemies. The 1975 Sinai II disengagement agreement he laboriously brokered between Israel and Egypt led, in little more than two years, to Egyptian president Anwar Sadat's remarkable visit to Jerusalem and then to the 1979 Israel-Egypt peace treaty. And the disengagement agreement he brokered between Israel and Hafez Assad kept the peace on the Golan Heights for the next three and a half decades.

For more than three decades, Kissinger's record of achievement in managing the Middle East remains one that none of his successors ever neared. When it came to handling the region, he wrote the book.

Yitzhak Rabin: The dove who armed Israel

Yitzhak Rabin's first three-year term as prime minister of Israel was vastly underrated. His second, far more famous one, was vastly overrated. Rabin's first premiership launched a peace process with Egypt. His second launched a peace process with the Palestinians. Their outcome was very different, largely because Yasser Arafat was not Anwar Sadat.

In 1974 Rabin inherited the most ominous security situation any Israeli prime minister had faced since the first bloody struggle to establish the state. When Moshe Dayan became minister of defense in 1967, he knew he inherited the most powerful army and air force in the Middle East, fresh and poised to strike. But seven years later, Rabin inherited an Israeli army that had lost more than four times as many soldiers in the Yom Kippur war as had died in the Six-Day War. Three thousand Israeli soldiers had died out of a total population of only three million. This was proportional to the U.S. losing 300,000 dead in a war of only three weeks: three times the death toll of the Korean and Vietnam wars combined.

Also, the previously invincible Israeli army found that the tank and close air support strike forces that had served it so well in 1956 and 1967 were obsolete. The handheld, wire-guided, anti-tank missiles and hand-held surface-to-air missiles supplied by the Soviet Union to Egypt and Syria had inflicted carnage on Israel's elite, irreplaceable pilots and tank crews. Still massively outnumbered in manpower, Israel had lost the long-term tactical superiority it needed to survive.

Rabin's solution was to look to the nation he had admired ever since studying and serving there as a young Israeli officer in the 1950s. President Gerald Ford and Secretary of State Kissinger were putting enormous pressure on Israel to withdraw from the western sections of the Suez canal. Dayan had been ready to contemplate such a move after the Six-Day War, arguing in vain to Golda Meir that Israel should not keep its front line on the canal in any case. Rabin came to the same conclusion, but he decided to get something for the concession.

Rabin's price for signing the 1975 Sinai II disengagement agreement was a U.S.-Israeli arms deal quite unlike any seen before.

More than any arms deal Israel had signed before, the 1975 deal transformed the nature of the Israeli armed forces. The Israeli air force had

"You Will Never Understand"

"They arranged for the scenes of the execution to be recorded: the prisoner led from the cell to the place of execution, the blindfolding, the order to fire, the blood pouring out of the mouth, the knees folding under the victim, his body leaning forward as the cords were loosened, his mouth open to kiss the earth his mother. I said nothing. I went out and an officer asked me gaily, 'How did you like it, Doctor?' I said, 'Is this the Ba'ath?' He said, 'I do not understand.' I said, 'You will never understand.'"

Sami al-Jundi, by then Syrian minister of information, describing the execution of supporters of Egyptian president Gamal Abdel Nasser after the unsuccessful coup attempt of July 18, 1963, in Damascus served as flying artillery for the army, providing the kind of close tactical ground support that proved so decisive for the U.S., British, Soviet, and German armies in the great land battles of World War II. But the heavy losses to simple surface-to-air guided missiles from poorly trained Egyptian and Syrian combat soldiers during the 1973 war proved that those days were over. Israel would have to rely on real heavy artillery now that its fabled "flying artillery" arm had been broken. Ford, Kissinger, and Schlesinger provided that artillery—the heaviest there was. They supplied every caliber of artillery heavy gun the Israelis needed, including massive 155 mm ones. Before the 1973 war, Israel's conventional artillery arm had been nonexistent. After the deal in 1975, it had the most powerful artillery in the Middle East.

The gifts in the gigantic $900 million package (more than $3.5 billion in today's dollars) also included a new generation of main battle tanks. In follow-up agreements, U.S. funding flowed to finance development and production of the Merkava (Hebrew for "chariot"), Israel's own home-produced main battle tank. Ford also agreed to supply Israel with the finest combat aircraft in the U.S. arsenal, the McDonnell Douglas F-15 Eagle.

The 1975 arms deal transformed the Israeli army in ways that continue to this day. It would no longer be the lightning-fast force of lightly armed elite troops attacking boldly by night, as envisioned by Orde Wingate and the blitzkrieg-influenced military commanders of the 1950s. It would now be a huge masse de materiel, more slow-moving but overwhelming in the firepower it could bring to bear. Rabin Americanized the Israeli army, and it remains so to this day.

Israeli pundits at the time and historians since have seen Rabin's first premiership as a study in weakness and ineffectualness. They could not have been more wrong As the *Jerusalem Post*'s Philip Gillon presciently noted at the time, Rabin showed a determination and readiness to make hard, crucial decisions worthy of David Ben-Gurion himself.

Ironically, it was the F-15 Eagles he so coveted for his country that brought Rabin down. In 1977, he held a proud ceremony at Israel's Ben-Gurion Airport to welcome the first of the F-15s from the United States. But it was a Friday afternoon and the aircraft were flying behind schedule. The ceremony stretched into the early hours of the Jewish Sabbath. Jewish religious parties Rabin depended on for his coalition majority in the Knesset pulled out of the government to protest the event running into the Sabbath. Their leaders expected the usually mild-mannered Rabin to simply practice business as usual and plead with them to come back. Instead, the infuriated prime minister resigned and called a general election. This led to the fall of his government and the end of the Labor Party's three-decade-long control of the Israeli state. Rabin had boasted in the welcoming ceremony for the F-15s that they would usher in a vastly changed Israel. Even he did not dream how vastly changed it would truly be.

Did Jimmy Carter really bring peace to the Middle East?

In four short years, President Jimmy Carter taught the world and his presidential successors an unfailing formula to wreck the Middle East: focus obsessively on bringing peace between the Israelis and the Palestinians, as if God chose only you and your personal "experts" to do it, and force friendly governments to slit their own throats by installing full-scale American-style democracy immediately. It fails every time.

Carter proved conclusively, as Britain's Neville Chamberlain had forty years before him, that the road to hell is paved with good intentions. A personally decent, honorable, incorruptible evangelical Christian, he wanted nothing more or less than to bring eternal peace between the Children of Abraham, the Jews and the Arabs.

Thanks to Gerald Ford and Henry Kissinger, Carter came into office with an awful lot going for him. Even so, his bungling, rather than his skill, gave him his big breakthrough. In 1977, Carter wanted the Soviet Union to be the United States' partner in running a Middle East peace conference or diplomatic initiative to settle the Israeli-Arab conflict. Egyptian president Anwar Sadat confronted the idea with understandable horror. He had risked his life and the future of his country to kick Nasser's Soviet advisors out in 1971. The last thing he needed was some extraordinarily naïve U.S. president letting them come back, bound for revenge. So the man who had confounded all expectations by expelling the Soviets six years earlier announced that within days he was going to visit Jerusalem.

The move was astounding beyond imagination. Nothing like it had ever been seen in the history of the Middle East. Sadat was going to meet the (supposedly) most hard-line, ferocious, and implacable Israeli leader of them all: Menachem Begin, whose Likud bloc had finally won power in the 1977 general elections after he had endured six previous electoral defeats in a row as leader of the Herut and Gahal parties.

Nor was Sadat just going to Tel Aviv, which would have been radical enough. He was going to Jerusalem, the city whose Islamic holy sites had been in Israeli hands for more than a decade, to the unending fury of the entire Arab and Muslim worlds.

Friends and enemies alike were stunned. General Mordechai Gur, the tough Israeli general who had led the forces that stormed the Old City in 1967, suspected a trap. Only Begin took the whole thing in stride. Thousands of reporters and television news teams flooded in from around the world. Bezeq, Israel's justly reviled nationalized telephone company, which usually couldn't install a simple phone in an apartment without a three-year delay, set up flawlessly working free global communications for all of them in less than a week.

Sadat's Jerusalem visit was the biggest thing of its kind since the Queen of Sheba had come to woo King Solomon. Sadat was less impressed. And there was certainly no love affair between Egypt and Israel to rival the famous biblical one. But they did share their hearts' desire: peace between their two countries and, for Sadat, a demand that the entire demilitarized Sinai Peninsula be returned to Egypt.

What followed was more than fifteen months of long, exhausting, mean, and obsessive negotiations. Carter threw himself into the heart of them and obsessed over every detail. (Like Herbert Hoover, Carter, who personally planned the schedules for the White House tennis court, thrived on details, the more useless the better.) Eventually, it all came together at the 1978 Camp David peace conference, where Carter basically locked up the sovereign leaders of Israel and Egypt in what amounted to a luxury prison, with the Secret Service as their jailers, until they finally agreed on a peace treaty.

The irony is that none of it was necessary, and that lasting peace between Israel and Egypt may well have been possible, on far more favorable terms for Israel, without it.

Sadat frankly refused to make peace without getting all of the Sinai back, but since Kissinger's monumental Sinai II agreement in 1975, he had the reality of peace anyway. The eventual treaty hammered out at Camp David was made possible only with enormous annual payments of more than $4 billion from the American taxpayer to Israel and Egypt alike. Israel got a little more than Egypt in absolute terms, but as it had a much smaller population, vastly more in per capita terms. But by giving up the Sinai, Israel lost the strategic depth it would desperately need if it made any long-term agreement with the Palestinians. It also lost the territory it would ultimately need if it ever faced an implacable enemy determined to acquire nuclear weapons. The more Israel's population was concentrated in the area of greater Tel Aviv, the more tempting it would be for any genocidal-minded maniac to wipe out the bulk of the population at a single stroke. By giving up the Sinai, Begin made that nightmare a lot easier to achieve.

Retaining much of Sinai would also have made it far easier to maintain control of the Gaza Strip. The Palestinians were adept, as the Viet Cong had been before them, in constructing endless arrays of tunnels to smuggle weapons into Gaza from Egypt when the Israeli-Egyptian border was right beside them. And in sharp contrast to Gaza and the West Bank, Sinai was almost uninhabited.

Far from bringing peace with its neighbors, there is a good argument to be made that Carter's work enabled Begin to start a disastrous war that his country has been paying for ever since. Peace with Egypt in the south

PC Myth: Ronald Reagan Didn't Know What He Was Doing

Everybody knew Henry Kissinger was a genius, and if they didn't, he never hesitated to tell them so. But President Ronald Reagan got equally impressive results by appearing to be so much less than he was.

When Reagan took office, the United States was reduced to an even lower state of humiliation and apparent impotence than it had been during the 1973–1974 oil embargo. The new Islamic revolutionary regime in Iran was still holding fifty-two American diplomats and other U.S. citizens hostage, and at home the national will to act still had not recovered from the traumas of Vietnam and Watergate.

Reagan succeeded by talking tough, acting cautiously, and planning brilliantly. He and his top officials not only restored and strengthened America's dominant position in the Middle East, but they even used it successfully to economically undermine the Soviet Union and send it sliding to disintegration.

Reagan recognized that the inefficient Soviet Communist system thrived on high global energy prices, just as they were a nightmare for the United States, Japan, and the other major industrialized nations of the free world. He therefore worked very closely with King Khaled and Crown

continued on next page

freed Begin to launch his army into Lebanon to the north in spring 1982. But Defense Minister Ariel Sharon's grand design for Lebanon quickly went disastrously wrong. Israel suffered hundreds of dead and thousands of wounded before it finally withdrew from much of southern Lebanon after a broken Begin left office.

Had Egypt remained essentially powerless and in the U.S. orbit, but without a final peace treaty with Israel, and had Israel maintained control of most of the Sinai, but forced to be on guard in the south, Begin would never have dared to open up an ambitious new front in the north.

continued from previous page

Prince Fahd of Saudi Arabia to ensure that U.S. military power protected the kingdom, both from the Soviets and from the Iranian revolutionaries across the Gulf who had just toppled the shah.

Reagan's conservative hero, Britain's wartime prime minister Winston Churchill, had not hesitated to support Soviet leader Josef Stalin, the most prolific killer in human history, when the Soviets were attacked by the even more dangerous threat of Nazi Germany in 1941. Reagan showed equal vision, boldness, and *realpolitik* cynicism in supporting the worst tyrant in the Middle East, Saddam Hussein, when Saddam attacked Iran in 1980. The Iranians rallied behind their charismatic leader, Ayatollah Khomeini, and the ensuing war dragged on for eight years. Under Reagan, the United States provided invaluable support to Saddam, including real-time intelligence on where the more numerous but slow-moving and tactically inept Iranian forces were planning to attack.

Reagan succeeded in all his major Middle East goals. He strengthened Israel, preserved Iraq, wooed Saudi Arabia, kept oil prices remarkably low, and ensured that the 1980s were a decade of global prosperity. America boomed as a result. The only place he stumbled was in Lebanon. But even there, he quickly learned from his mistakes, sacked the people responsible, and avoided getting sucked into a war he did not want. His brilliant example deserves far closer study from his successors than it has received.

He and Sharon might still have swept the PLO out of the large enclave it controlled in southern Lebanon, but they would never have dared to push on into the heart of Lebanon. Hezbollah, created by this series of maneuvers, proved a far more formidable and long-lasting enemy of the Jewish state than the PLO had ever been.

The Israeli-Egyptian peace treaty also cost America the life of its most important and constructive ally in the entire Middle East. On October 6, 1981, Anwar Sadat proudly reviewed his armed forces as they marched past him in massed array. A small group of Islamic extremist conspirators in his own army, furious at Sadat's peace with Israel, broke ranks as their unit marched by the reviewing stand and stormed it, their automatic rifles blazing. Sadat died instantly. His fate was sealed by the most enormous decoration he wore on his chest: the Star of Sinai. It was just too big and garish to miss.

Had the 1975 Sinai II disengagement agreement been allowed to define Israeli-Egyptian relations, Sadat would have lived and extreme Islamism would never have won its greatest assassination coup to date. But by then, the other supposed great ally of the United States in the Middle East had also fallen, even more a victim to Carter's romantic and farcical sense of priorities. Carter's "great achievement" of peace between Israel and Egypt came at a disastrous price: it resulted in Iran's fall to Ayatollah Khomeini, launching a virulent new form of Islamist extremism hitherto inconceivable. From November 1977 through March 1979, Carter was so obsessed with achieving an Israeli-Egyptian peace treaty that he ignored the increasing evidence that the shah of Iran's position was crumbling with amazing speed.

Clinton: Carter all over again

At first glance, Bill Clinton's dealings with the Middle East appeared the absolute opposite of the hapless Carter's experience. And compared with many of the bungles the subsequent Bush administration would make, it arguably still looks good.

Under Clinton, peace and relative stability were preserved throughout the region, and the Israeli-Palestinian peace process seemed to advance. Even Iran appeared to become more moderate, with the 1997 election of the remarkably moderate (at least by Islamic Republic standards) Mohammad Khatami. And oil prices until 1999 stayed astonishingly low. Compared to Carter's nightmarish record of buffoonish incompetence, this was a welcome contrast indeed.

But as it turned out, Clinton repeated Carter's basic mistake of focusing obsessively on the Israeli-Arab peace process. He shared Carter's megalomaniacal delusion that he could forge the lasting peace that had eluded previous generations on either side. As a result, like Carter, Clinton and his top experts on the region ignored or catastrophically underrated the remorseless—but otherwise highly preventable—rise of a ferocious enemy that would kill more Americans in a single day than the Japanese navy did at Pearl Harbor.

Clinton cannot take either credit or blame for the Oslo Peace Process. It was former Israeli super-hawk (now turned ultra-dove) Shimon Peres who laid that egg. And it was Rabin—haunted by memories of the death cries of his young comrades in the 1947 fighting for Jerusalem—who made the crucial decision to go along with Peres.

But once Rabin and Arafat held that famous meeting and shook hands on the White House lawn in 1993, Clinton and his team eagerly jumped aboard the "Peace at Last" express. Where Carter had obsessively thrown himself into every nook and cranny of the Israeli-Egyptian negotiations for eighteen months, Clinton did so for a full seven years. The climax came in July 2000 when, with the sands of time running out on his second term, Clinton convened a Camp David II peace summit with Israeli prime minister Ehud Barak and the old and ailing Arafat.

Using Jimmy Carter as a model for anything, even for what still appeared to be his one undisputed great diplomatic achievement, should have given the Clinton team pause, but clearly it did not. The idea and driving force for the conference reportedly came from Barak, who capped a brilliant career as Israel's top special forces commander (during which his exploits exceeded even those of Dayan and Sharon) with a short and utterly bungled premiership. But there is no doubt that Clinton and his top peace negotiators were exceptionally eager to make the effort.

For such an ambitious endeavor, Barak and his team bungled the staff work for Camp David II abysmally. It is difficult to imagine that the man who had been the legendary commander of special forces and then a respected IDF chief of staff could have proven so sloppy in preparing for his greatest challenge as national leader.

But Barak, as his intimates later revealed, did not even do the basic diplomatic preparation of sounding out the Palestinians' absolute bottom-line terms for a settlement. What he offered was, from the Israeli perspective, immensely generous: more than 90 percent of the West Bank. But he didn't yield on the right of return for the descendents of Palestinian refugees from the 1947 war, about which Arafat was insistent. He also insisted on maintaining total Israeli control over the entire city of Jerusalem, and on retaining the relatively small amount of territory beyond the 1967 borders on which 180,000 Israelis had built towns and settlements. This was 80 percent of the total Israeli settler population beyond the Green Line.

Over the previous seven years, Arafat had gained a vast amount for himself, and had made his first gains for his long-suffering people, by compromising for the first time in his life. But at Camp David II, when he could have won so much more, he turned it down. Demanding nothing but the entire cake, he lost the much larger slice of it he would otherwise have had. His decision was true to the patterns of bizarre behavior and logic that had governed his entire life. It also condemned Israelis and

Palestinians alike to a new round of war and suffering greater than anything they had endured in more than fifty years.

For Clinton, the failure of Camp David II dashed his dreams of securing a lasting and secure peace for both sides. But worse by far, Clinton and his chief Middle East peace envoy, Dennis Ross, had forgotten the lasting wisdom of Henry Kissinger: when disputes are not resolvable, it is best to recognize what cannot be resolved and simply concentrate on improving the conditions that can be improved. Eventually, conditions and attitudes may change sufficiently to reconcile the previously irreconcilable, but trying to do too much too soon always backfires.

That was the consequence of Camp David II. When Ariel Sharon visited the Temple Mount in September 2000, an admittedly potentially incendiary move, Arafat used it to set off a new Palestinian intifada. The First Intifada had been fought with violent but non-lethal protests, because guns and explosives were not easily available on the West Bank and in Gaza after twenty years of effective Israeli control. The Second Intifada was far more lethal.

Some 1,100 Israeli civilians died in the following four years of mayhem, and probably at least three times that number of Palestinians died from Israeli retaliation. Rabin's idealism and Peres's utopian visions had born bitter fruit.

The United States bore a worse and more direct price. In the years before Camp David II, and in the fevered months up to, during, and after it, Clinton and his top officials paid no attention to the mounting evidence that al Qaeda, a once obscure but increasingly formidable extreme Islamist terrorist group led by Saudi renegade Osama bin Laden, had become emboldened. Encouraged by its previous impunity from retaliation by the U.S. armed forces, it was now preparing a terrorist attack of unprecedented scale on the two of the greatest cities in the United States.

Chapter 9

THE HISTORY OF SEPTEMBER 11

The terrorist attacks of September 11, 2001, had a profound effect on the American psyche. The story of that day, what led up to it, and what resulted from it is slowly starting to solidify. It sometimes seems the only people questioning the official version are the "truthers"—the Michael Moore types convinced that somehow Bush and Halliburton, together with the Carlyle Group and probably Wal-Mart, staged the attack.

But the official history of September 11 has been infested by political correctness, and we do need to set the record straight. Mostly, it's important to remember the bungling of the Clinton administration and the cover-ups by Clinton's national security advisor Sandy Berger. Also, it's crucial to debunk conspiracy theories about Saudi involvement; one of bin Laden's goals was to weaken Saudi Arabia by harming U.S.-Saudi ties. We also need to squelch the claims of the blame-America-firsters. Osama bin Laden and his pawns are the only people responsible for September 11.

Clinton's team missed the al Qaeda threat

It's crucial for the Left to claim that under Clinton Americans enjoyed years of peace and prosperity. The economy grew, they say, and government

Guess what?

- Officials in both the CIA and FBI knew that al Qaeda posed a grave threat, but because of bureaucratic red tape, they weren't allowed to share information.

- Turning the U.S. against the Saudis was a key element of Osama bin Laden's September 11 plot.

spending was even kept under control. They admit Clinton may have had personal shortcomings, but he governed well. To preserve this myth, you need to believe that September 11 came out of nowhere, with no warning at all. To believe that, you need to ignore history.

Al Qaeda was hardly unknown to U.S. policymakers before September 11. It had already carried out two ambitious and devastating attacks on U.S. targets, well outside the normal range of Middle Eastern terror groups. On August 7, 1998, the group simultaneously bombed the U.S. embassies in Nairobi, Kenya, and Dar es Salaam, Tanzania. Together, 223 people were killed and more than 4,000 were wounded. I and many other American journalists correctly ascribed the bombings to al Qaeda at the time. The name was apparently first publicly used (spelled al-Qaida) by President Bill Clinton only two weeks after these attacks.

On October 12, 2000, al Qaeda members using nothing more high-tech than a rowboat filled with explosives severely damaged the USS *Cole* in Aden, Yemen. Seventeen U.S. sailors were killed and another thirty-nine were injured. The group was clearly already competent, and dangerous. The attacks on the embassies showed a capability to organize ambitious simultaneous attacks against different targets.

It later emerged that different parts of the enormous U.S. international intelligence and domestic security organizations had received disparate pieces of information indicating that al Qaeda was organizing attacks within the United States itself. This was something that neither the PLO, Black September, and or any other Palestinian terror group had dared or been able to do.

A number of senior U.S. officials were alert to the dangers al Qaeda posed. One was Richard Clarke, who was in charge of counter-terrorism in the Clinton administration, which Clinton rightly made a cabinet-level job. Another was John O'Neill, a brilliant, abrasive, go-getting deputy director at the FBI who was forced out of office in 2000 because he made slick, useless bureaucrats uncomfortable. A third was George Tenet, Clinton's own director of Central Intelligence. To his credit, George W. Bush kept both Tenet and Clarke in their positions—highly unusual for any incoming opposition president. (Clarke's position was downgraded.)

However, what followed was a bipartisan catastrophe. Clinton and his National Security Council team, headed by national security advisor Sandy Berger, never took the threat of al Qaeda seriously enough. After September 11, well after the Clinton administration left office, Berger, in an unprecedented and highly improper series of clearly premeditated actions between September 2 and October 2, 2003, withdrew hundreds of pages of documents dealing with Islamist terror threats to the United States from the U.S. National Archives in Washington. Many of those documents were never returned, and Berger, after contradicting himself in previous accounts, eventually admitted to destroying many of them. On September 8, 2005, he was fined $50,000 and sentenced to one hundred hours of community service for these actions. Considering that the documents he destroyed might well have served as evidence for impeachment against him by some future U.S. Congress, the penalty seems a cheap price for him to pay. It seems a reasonable presumption to conclude that Berger

Books You're Not Supposed to Read

The catastrophes of September 11 have produced a library of books, many of them very good. Two of the very best are *Against All Enemies: Inside America's War on Terror* by Richard Clarke; New York: Free Press, 2004, and *The Looming Tower: Al Qaeda and the Road to September 11* by Lawrence Wright; New York: Vintage, 2007.

No one was in a better position than Clarke to write the inside story on the repeated bungles of top-level U.S. policymakers under both Clinton and Bush. Abrasive, opinionated, knowledgeable, honest, and outspoken, he wrote that rare thing, a Washington memoir that carries conviction. It is also a gripping read.

So is Wright's book, focused as it is on the tragic hero John J. O'Neill, who could have stopped the September 11 terror plot in its tracks. But no one else put the pieces together, and like Clarke, O'Neill was shrugged off by the suits in both the Clinton and Bush administrations as being too hardcharging. What that meant was that he was hardworking, dynamic, intelligent, honest, and determined to protect his country.

destroyed the documents because they contained exceptionally incriminating or embarrassing evidence about how he and top Clinton officials underestimated al Qaeda.

Bush drops the ball on al Qaeda too

Unfortunately, the incoming Bush administration was just as complacent. A frustrated John O'Neill was squeezed out of the FBI. His repeated warnings about catastrophe on the horizon had discredited him in the complacent eyes of policymakers and movers and shakers in both parties. He took a job running security for the World Trade Center and was in his office on the thirty-fourth floor when the hijacked airliner struck his building. He survived the initial blast and called his family to tell them he was all right. But he insisted on going to back to help rescue others, and perished when the towers collapsed. He was one of the most heroic and certainly the most tragic figure in the whole business.

Meanwhile, able officials at both the FBI and the CIA were restricted from sharing information and cooperating effectively by congressional legislation passed in the post-Vietnam era by Democratic-controlled Congresses. ACLU-inspired queasiness about intelligence gathering kept us from acting before September 11.

As late as September 10, Defense Secretary Donald Rumsfeld told a group of U.S. senators who wanted to switch $500 million—a relatively small sum by twenty-first-century defense budget standards—from high-tech weapons, including ballistic missile defense, to anti-terrorist operations that he would urge President Bush to veto any such measure. Nor is there any real indication, despite much subsequent spin to the contrary, that either Bush or Condoleezza Rice took George Tenet's warnings about al Qaeda's growing capabilities and evident intentions to carry out terror attacks within the United States any more seriously. Tenet tried to serve both Clinton and Bush decently, competently, and honorably. But if there was one charge that can be tellingly made against him, as a respected former senior congressional official who dealt with many of these issues told me, it was that he sometimes shrank from telling truth to power.

Thousands of Americans were about to die because of all the complacency, incompetence, and bungling.

Heroes and lessons

Only one high-tech system worked effectively to save thousands of American lives on September 11, and it didn't take a cent from the $360 billion Pentagon budget. That system was the ordinary cell phones passengers on United Airlines Flight 93 from Newark, New Jersey, to San Francisco used to report that their plane had been hijacked. Realizing they were on a one-way trip, and with nothing left to lose, several passengers informed their loved ones they were going to storm the hijackers, who had already slit the throats of the airline pilots, as their co-plotters did on the other three planes. No one will ever know the details of what followed, but the passengers succeeded in their goal: the airliner crashed into a Pennsylvania field, killing everyone on board. Its intended target appears to have been the United States Capitol, where the U.S. Senate and House of Representatives were both in session at the time.

Had that aspect of the plot succeeded, a national catastrophe would have escalated into a national crisis. What saved

Bin Laden Warned Us

In his March 1997 interview with CNN's Peter Arnett, Osama bin Laden appeared to refer directly to the attacks of September 11:

PETER ARNETT: What are your future plans?

BIN LADEN: You'll see them and hear about them in the media, God willing.

the nation from such an unprecedented crisis was the heroism and self-sacrifice of a handful of ordinary people.

The two hijacked planes targeted for the Twin Towers both hit their targets. They were not remotely controlled, as some more creative conspiracy nuts later claimed: a United Press International correspondent in Manhattan reported later how he observed with his own eyes that the hijacker pilot of the second airliner had corrected his flight to try to hit the tower at a lower point, to trap more people.

The towers were supposed to be able to withstand any aircraft crashing into them. Their steel structures, in fact, withstood the kinetic shocks of the two airliners, exactly as they were supposed to. But the towers had been designed before the first wide-body and "jumbo" airliners, and the hijackers had deliberately planned to hijack planes at the beginning of their cross-country flights so that their fuel tanks were still almost full.

Osama bin Laden had trained as a civilian engineer, and he boasted later that he had calculated that the intense heat of the burning gasoline would prove sufficient to melt the towers' steel structures. The two buildings were also more vulnerable because, in a design exceptionally unusual for any skyscraper, their steel skeletons had been erected on the outside, rather than in their inner core. Had the Twin Towers been built in the traditional manner, they might have survived.

The fourth hijacked plane was crashed into the Pentagon. The superiority of World War II architectural planning instead of 1960s skyscrapers approved by the Rockefellers was rapidly demonstrated. The Pentagon death toll was just above 200, a fraction of the 2,750 who died in the Twin Towers. The Pentagon

A Book You're Not Supposed to Read

For documentation of the serial incompetence and blindness of the Clinton administration on the subject, the book to read is *Breakdown: How America's Intelligence Failures Led to 9/11* by Bill Gertz; Washington, DC: Regnery, 2002. Gertz, the veteran intelligence correspondent at the *Washington Times*, produced a slam-dunk authoritative, devastating, and overwhelming in its documentation and detail.

doesn't even appear to have been the intended target. The hijiackers appear to have sought to destroy the White House, but they didn't realize that the White House is carefully camouflaged from aerial recognition and has been for years. Unable to identify the White House, they then struck the Pentagon as the most easily identifiable target, assuming that their comrades on United 93 would destroy the Capitol.

Defense Secretary Rumsfeld showed—or appeared to show—great coolness and self-confidence when visiting the site of the crashed airliner in his own Pentagon headquarters. However, later reports revealed that Rumsfeld may not have been fully aware of what was going on or how to respond. He spent the rest of that fateful morning painstakingly drafting legal rules of engagement under which the U.S. Air Force could shoot down hijacked airliners.

The Saudis weren't complicit in the attacks

Catastrophes and assassinations always produce conspiracy theories, most of them absurd, and September 11 was no exception. War hawks who wanted to invade Iraq tried to hang the blame on Saddam Hussein. There wasn't a shred of real evidence to support that contention, though deputy defense secretary Paul Wolfowitz was urging an invasion of Iraq within twenty-four hours of the attacks.

At the other end of the spectrum were the left-wing nuts led by Michael Moore, who always had hated the Saudis because they were rich, conservative, religious, traditional, and—worst of all—friends of the United States and the Bush family.

Most of the hijackers were indeed Saudis, the rest were Egyptians. This was no accident. Bin Laden wanted to torpedo the U.S.-Saudi alliance, so he wanted as many Saudi nationals as possible implicated in the attack. He was determined to reestablish the caliphate that Mustafa Kemal Ataturk had abolished in 1924, and his first and primary targets were the rulers of his own nation, whom he hated with a virulent passion. The Saudis' main source of income remained their oil exports, and U.S. military support remained essential to the kingdom's survival in the face of the Iranian and Iraqi threats. Therefore, bin Laden's strategic goal on September 11, beyond slaughtering thousands of Americans and decapitating the entire U.S. political system, was to destroy the U.S.-Saudi alliance. He didn't quite succeed, but in the short term, he damaged it badly.

The Heroics of Flight 93

The hijackers of Flight 93 had warned the passengers to stay still, but once they learned that jets had crashed into the Twin Towers and the Pentagon, they realized they needed to take action. Below is an excerpt of the cell phone conversation between Flight 93 passenger Tom Burnett and his wife, Deena:

TOM: We're waiting until we're over a rural area. We're going to take back the airplane.

DEENA: No! Sit down, be still, be quiet, and don't draw attention to yourself! [the exact words taught to her by Delta Airlines flight attendant training]

TOM: Deena, if they're going to crash this plane into the ground, we're going to have to do something.

DEENA: What about the authorities?

TOM: We can't wait for the authorities. I don't know what they could do anyway. It's up to us. I think we can do it.

DEENA: What do you want me to do?

TOM: Pray, Deena, just pray.

DEENA: [after a long pause] I love you.

TOM: Don't worry, we're going to do something.

Bin Laden was a renegade, but he was a renegade from one of the wealthiest, best-connected, most influential, and most respected families in Saudi Arabia. Immediately after September 11, the Saudis reacted by rushing as many of their notables out of the United States as possible. Later extensive research gave no indication that any significant figures in the Saudi royal family, government, or major institutions were involved in the plot, but the mass flight did play into the hands of conspiracy mongers. Much damage was also done by Michael Moore's immensely popular documentary *Fahrenheit 9/11*. In the year before the 2004 presidential election the movie made more than $100 million—an unprecedented achievement for any American documentary on theatrical release, though the secret of its success was the anti-Saudi and anti–oil company paranoia with which Moore laced it.

The United States paid a heavy price for the anti-Saudi paranoia fanned by Moore and his friends. The Saudis were alarmed by all the rhetoric, and they feared that the tough measures in the USA PATRIOT Act that could freeze terrorist capital could freeze Saudi capital as well. They moved most of the liquid assets they had kept for decades in the United States to other parts of the world. No one knows the exact sums involved, but estimates have run as high as many billions of dollars.

Why did it happen?

Weakening Saudi Arabia was a major aim of bin Laden, but he had no shortage of reasons to hate the U.S. Self-hating Americans like to say bin Laden attacked the U.S. because we oppressed the Palestinians, or because of our capitalist greed. Others blame our corrupt culture or our military overreach. In some ways, they're all right: bin Laden attacked us because of everything about us.

If you look at bin Laden's various public statements, before and after September 11, you see that the list of complaints is long. In 1996, after he issued his "Declaration of War Against the Americans Who Occupy" Saudi Arabia, he attributed the jihad to the fact that the U.S. government is "unjust, criminal, and tyrannical." He cited American "support for the Israeli occupation," as well as our finance industry (charging interest, you know), and our consumption of alcohol. In a post–September 11 statement, he attacked the U.S. for our blockade against Saddam Hussein's regime, Israel's use of force against the Palestinians, the bombing of Hiroshima and Nagasaki, and the very existence of Israel.

Very simply, the only way we could have avoided the attack was by preventing it through intelligence and counter-terrorism measures.

Chapter 10

PEACE IN THE MIDDLE EAST
WHAT WORKS, AND WHAT DOESN'T

Can anything be done about the Middle East? Can peace be attained? Can we leave them alone, and hope they don't bother us?

Jimmy Carter and George Bush have shown us that good intentions and Western liberal ideals won't solve Middle East's problems. Indeed, they tend to make things worse. This has caused some Americans to call for us to isolate ourselves from the region and let them fight it out themselves. That might have worked—had Jews never settled in the region and had oil never been discovered.

The Middle East is a mess, but not a hopeless mess. Looking at the region today, we can see what works and what doesn't work.

Hope at the end of the millennium

At the end of the twentieth century, the immediate prospects for the Middle East looked hopeful. Saddam Hussein still ruled in Iraq and Hafez Assad in Syria, but Saddam had no influence outside Iraq, and Assad was playing it cautious. Even Iran had a relatively moderate leader, President Mohammad Khatami, and the religious anti-Western fervor of the Islamic Revolution seemed to be running out of steam. Khatami even offered

Guess what?

⚜ The world's food supply depends on oil to make fertilizers to protect crops. Without oil, more than two billion people would starve to death.

⚜ Even if Israel were destroyed, extreme Islamists would still want to conquer the West.

⚜ The key to a stable Middle East is not a democratic Iraq but a powerful Saudi Arabia.

195

Presidents Bill Clinton and George W. Bush a deal to scrap his nuclear program in return for diplomatic relations and an end to confrontation, but neither president dared to grasp that particular nettle. Khatami's attempts at relative moderation got nowhere, and in 2005, a very different man replaced him as leader of Iran: Mahmoud Ahmadinejad.

Ahmadinejad's emergence was only one in a series of grim developments that made the Middle East a vastly more ominous and threatening place at the beginning of the twenty-first century than it had been just a few short years before.

Oil prices, which had been lower than ten dollars a barrel in 1999, had climbed to more than ninety dollars a barrel by late 2007. Saddam and Assad were both gone, but things were vastly worse in both countries than when the two grim old Ba'athists were still alive. In Iraq, U.S. forces quickly toppled Saddam, and at the end of 2006 he was deservedly hanged for just a fraction of the monstrous crimes he had committed. But U.S. policymakers, saddled with liberal, do-gooder dreams about equality and democracy, bungled the peace. In 2006 and 2007, more Iraqis were dying and at a faster rate than they had during the awful Saddam years.

In Syria, Assad's son Bashar ruled securely as president, but he proved far more threatening than his cautious father had. Syria bought new missiles from Russia, and by 2007 Israeli military analysts judged the danger of an outbreak of direct war between Syria and Israel greater than at any time since 1973.

Under Ahmadinejad, a man who publicly denied the Holocaust, Iran pushed ahead with its nuclear armament development program faster than ever before. Ahmadinejad openly boasted of annihilating Israel. The threat of an Israeli or American preemptive strike against the Iranian nuclear facilities steadily grew.

The Palestinian-Israeli situation also saw some bad turns at the turn of the millennium. In 2000, Yasser Arafat refused to accept major Israeli concessions at the Camp David II peace conference and then unleashed a bloody new terror assault on Israel. Before dying, he went back to what he knew best: fighting. Beginning in 2000, the second Palestinian intifada shook Israel for five years, with its main tactic suicide bomb attacks against civilians in public places. More Israeli civilians died during Arafat's last hurrah than in any previous conflict except for the 1948 war. Arafat appears to have genuinely believed that Israel would fall apart under the assault. Instead, Israelis rallied together. Arafat's old arch-antagonist Ariel Sharon became prime minister at last and enjoyed his finest hour. He held his country together and responded ferociously in retaliatory strikes against both Gaza and the West Bank. The Israelis kept killing off Hamas leaders, but it didn't do any good. The French had found the same thing when they targeted the National Liberation Front's high command during the Algerian war of independence. What did eventually work, however, was building huge defenses to cut off most of the West Bank and Gaza from Israel.

By 2007, there was a good case to be made that the Middle East had indeed finally become the world's most dangerous neighborhood. The irony was that, despite its reputation, it had never been so before.

They are here to stay

When we look at the difficulty of setting up a stable democracy in Iraq, many Americans assert that the Middle East is nearly incapable of permanent or legitimate government. Respected journalist Charles Glass, hardly an unconditional admirer of the United States and Israel, called the countries of the region "tribes with flags." And it is certainly the case in the early twenty-first century that the new wave of Islamist extremism, enflamed by the disastrously bungled U.S. military commitment in Iraq, put previously stable regimes like those of Jordan, Saudi Arabia, and Egypt at new risk.

The fact remains that by the beginning of the twenty-first century the nation-states of Egypt, Syria, Jordan, Saudi Arabia, and even Iraq had all been in their current borders and essential form for more than seventy-five years each. That makes them older than three-quarters of the member states of the United Nations. Most of the nations of the Arab League had won their independence before India and Pakistan became independent nations in 1947 and before the People's Republic of China was established in 1949. The major oil-producing states, with the exception of Iraq (Saddam's murderous bungles again), have proven far more generous, socially just, and skillful at sharing their vast wealth with their people and maintaining social stability. Compare that to other oil majors around the world, such as Venezuela, Iran (where the shah went under), or Indonesia, which under the long rule of President Suharto was probably the most corrupt nation on earth.

Even Gamal Abdel Nasser's regime in Egypt, the most militarily incompetent government in modern Middle East history, didn't fall after three consecutive humiliations at Israel's hands—the 1956 Sinai Campaign, the 1967 Six-Day War, and the 1969–1970 War of Attrition. The Second Ba'ath Republic in Iraq retained its implacable, terrible grip on power from 1968 until total military defeat at the hands of the United States toppled it in 2003. And against all the prognostications of American pundits both old and new, the Ba'ath Republic in Syria has endured since 1970. Even little Jordan, established as a casual afterthought by Winston Churchill during his holiday amid the Pyramids at the Cairo Conference in 1921, continues to thrive under King Abdullah II, though there is no doubt Hamas has it firmly in its sights. And so far, the endless prophecies of doom that have been thrown at the shrewd and cautious House of Saud over the past half-century have not been worth a cent.

This obvious record of political and even social achievement should have given the ambitious armchair strategists of the first Bush administration, who dreamed of redrawing the map of the Middle East, cause for pause. Unfortunately, it didn't.

Arab democracy = extremist rule

After the attacks of September 11 killed three thousand Americans, it became fashionable in the Bush administration and U.S. pundit circles to talk about "draining the swamp" of the Middle East by forcing corrupt, supposedly out-of-touch regimes to initiate crash-democratization reforms. A key figure in persuading Bush administration policymakers to embrace this idea was Natan Sharansky, the former Israeli refusenik hero who had defied more than a decade of imprisonment and abuse by the Soviet KGB to emerge as a Jewish hero. He eventually became a political leader and right-wing government minister in Israel. Sharansky's book *The Case for Democracy* and his embrace of this argument proved enormously influential with President George W. Bush and Secretary of State Condoleezza Rice, who sought to enforce it at the beginning of Bush's second term in 2005. The results were uniformly disastrous for the United States and its many friends and allies in the region.

Islamic extremists and ferociously anti-American parties and movements made huge gains in elections in Kuwait and Egypt. Hamas won legislative elections in Gaza that the United States had pressured Palestinian Authority president Mahmoud Abbas to hold. Wherever genuinely free democratic elections were held across the region, extreme Islamist parties were immensely strengthened.

There should have been no surprise at any of this. Democracies are far from always peaceful. During its first forty years of popular democracy after 1828, the United States expanded across half a continent and fought the bloodiest civil war in modern Western history. The greatest growth of the British Empire across all of Africa and the Middle East came only after universal male suffrage was introduced in 1867.

Far from "draining the swamp," the policy of undermining authoritarian or cautiously conservative regimes was much more akin to blowing apart the watertight doors on the *Titanic*. The example of Saudi Arabia since September 11 shows that strong, traditional, and stable governments in the Sunni Muslim Middle East, given reasonable stability across their borders, are perfectly capable of suppressing Islamic extremism and terrorism. Indeed, they are a lot better at doing it than the United States and its armed forces have proven to be in Iraq.

In the year after September 11 the most valuable intelligence the United States received in its fight against al Qaeda came from the secret services of Jordan and Syria. (The Israeli intelligence simply wasn't very good.) But the Syrians became furious at the Bush administration's continuing hostility to them and broke off that valuable cooperation.

Still, politicians in both parties talk as if functioning democracy in Iraq can solve our problems in the region. The facts on the ground suggest something very different: the character of Islam and the Arab people requires tough, autocratic government like Saudi Arabia—or the Ottoman Empire.

Why solving the Israeli-Palestinian conflict won't solve the problems

There is no doubt that the Arab world and the wider Muslim community is enflamed by continued Israeli control of the holy places in Jerusalem, and by the very continued existence of the Jewish state. As we have seen, this has been the case ever since Haj Amin al-Husseini, the mufti of Jerusalem between the world wars, succeeded so well in Islamicizing his local, bitter conflict with the infant Jewish community in Palestine.

For seventy years, ambitious peacemakers, especially Americans and Israelis with visions of Nobel Peace Prizes dancing in their heads, have pursued a two-state solution like the pot of gold at the end of the rainbow. The unending nature of the conflict has convinced more than a few people in the West that wider peace in the region can come only through a lasting Israeli-Palestinian peace settlement.

Such a perfect, just, and fair deal satisfying every side would certainly be nice. But with Hamas taking over in Gaza—a development encouraged by bungled Israeli and U.S. policies in the region over the past fifteen years—that development looks further away and more unlikely than ever. But even if it could be achieved, the threat of an extreme Islamist takeover of major Arab nations, including the wealthiest ones, wouldn't vanish overnight. And if Israel were somehow destroyed either by Iranian nuclear attack or by combined Syrian-Palestinian or Hezbollah-Iranian military action, Islamist confidence and power—and the dangers they pose to the United States and Western Europe—would get vastly worse, not better.

The reason for this is a simple and obvious one that Osama bin Laden understood very clearly. With a cynical clarity worthy of Niccolo Machiavelli or Adolf Hitler, he wrote that people like to follow a strong horse. He was right.

The whole history of the Arab world and the modern Middle East recorded in this book confirms that when Western free market democracies militarily conquered and then occupied the region, the ruling elites wanted to be like them. When fascist or Communist nations seemed to be on the upswing against the West, copying them became the fashion in shaping Middle Eastern political parties and then running nation-states. Extreme Islam, not the religion as it has traditionally been practiced for at least seven hundred years, was concocted by Ayatollah Khomeini in Iran and Sayyid Qutb in Egypt. But if Hamas, Syria, and their Iranian allies somehow managed to destroy Israel, would al Qaeda magically disappear from the scene? Would the extreme Islamist terror threat to the United States and Western Europe vanish overnight? It is easy to see that it would not.

Radical Islam would be emboldened, not satisfied, by the destruction of Israel. Terror attacks and the extreme Islamist leaders' demands on the nations of Western Europe would increase, not decrease. Eliminating Israel would lead to a rapid increase in the popularity and prestige of extreme Islamic movements within previously far more moderate Muslim communities around the world. The best way to eliminate popular support for such groups remains to starve them of success.

When Adolf Hitler succeeded in conquering or otherwise absorbing all German majority regions in Europe into his Third Reich, he did not become a satisfied, peace-loving moderate. Instead, he accelerated his plans to invade Poland the following year. And when he succeeded in wiping out the French army and sweeping the British army off the European mainland in summer 1940, he did not seek the end of the war. Instead, he pushed ahead with planning his greatest crimes: the genocide of the Jewish people in Europe and the conquest and enslavement of the peoples of the Soviet Union.

Destroying Israel, therefore, would not magically eradicate anti-Western and anti-American sentiment from the Middle East. It would expand it to tidal-wave proportions, and the dark forces responsible would probably sweep to power across the region, destroying overnight traditionally moderate and responsible governments in countries like Egypt, Jordan, Saudi Arabia, and the Gulf States. This does not mean Western nations should abandon the Israeli-Palestinian conflict. But they should abandon their traditional dream of bringing an eternal, just, and lasting end to it.

Henry Kissinger's pessimistic wisdom in dealing with the conflict after the 1973 Yom Kippur War is now more appropriate than ever: there are conflicts that can be contained and allowed to die of old age, as the history of the Protestant-Catholic struggles in Northern Ireland demonstrates. The best thing that can be done is to try to ameliorate suffering and immediate grievances and provide security on both sides, while postponing the most difficult issues to a later date.

Assume that some "perfect" Israeli-Palestinian peace could be achieved between Israel and the Palestinians. Or even that Israel and the leaders of Hamas could reach a grudging but verifiable compromise. Would all the other social, religious, political, terror, economic, and security problems of the Middle East vanish overnight? They certainly would not.

It is striking to recall that when bin Laden and his allies got al Qaeda up and running in the 1990s, they paid almost no attention to the Israeli-Palestinian conflict. It simply wasn't important to them. They demanded the restoration of the caliphate to politically and religiously rule all Muslims, pure and simple. It would be a caliphate armed with nuclear weapons, controlling all the main oil-producing areas on earth. It would not be a peace-seeking or an accommodating one, as the Ottoman sultan-caliphs eventually became after they were thrown back from the gates of Vienna for the second time in 1683.

Bin Laden—and the extreme Islamist groups that have mushroomed across southern, southeastern, and central Asia over the past decade and a half—strive toward a militant, extreme caliphate that would make the nations of East and West alike bow down at its feet. They envision a supreme government, relentless in uniting the entire world under its own vision of Islam.

Establishing a lasting, fair, and just peace agreement between Israel and the Palestinians would not eliminate the grinding poverty of Egypt. It would not end the ambitions of al Qaeda to destroy the kingdom of Saudi Arabia and use all its oil wealth to finance endless, unlimited, jihad around the world. It would not end the efforts of 400,000 poor Yemenis a year to try to sneak into Saudi Arabia, adding to the large, potentially

The Ethanol Economy

We could conceivably replace or gasoline consumption with E-85, a fuel consisting of 85 percent ethanol. The country might look a little different, though:

> "By the year 2012, all the available cropland of the United States would be required for corn production.... By 2048, virtually the whole country, with the exception of cities, would be covered by corn plantations."

Marcelo E. Dias de Oliveira, et al., "Ethanol as Fuel: Energy, Carbon Dioxide Balances, and Ecological Footprint," *BioScience*, July 2005

threatening, unstable underclass in that country. It would not end the ambitions of the Islamic Republic of Iran to control the entire Gulf. Nor would it end or alleviate in any way the continuing anarchic chaos in Iraq.

The bloodiest conflict in modern Middle East history—the eight-year Iran-Iraq War—had nothing to do with the Israeli-Palestinian conflict at all. And when Syrian president Hafez Assad obliterated his own city of Hama, he did so to kill Islamists, not Jews.

The American pipe dream: A world without oil

The United States still imports twenty million barrels of oil a day, and China imports 5.6 million and rising fast. India is heading toward huge imports as well. Yet the idea of a "hydrogen economy" remains a fantasy. Hydrogen-powered automobiles are years, probably decades, away from being cheap, safe, and cost-effective. Ethanol, of course, is completely unprofitable without mammoth subsidies, and expanding it beyond a niche fuel would involve covering the nation with corn. The idea of getting the U.S., much less the planet, off oil is a pipe dream.

We need oil not only to power our cars and heat our homes, but also to make plastics (like your kitchen utensils or your desk chair) and to grow food, as well as transport it. Many plastics are "petroleum distillates," meaning their raw ingredient is black gold. If tree-hugging environmentalists want to continue the impressive protection and growth of forested areas in the Northern Hemisphere and finally get a handle on the continued catastrophic depletion of the rain forests of South America, sub-Saharan Africa, and Southeast Asia, then they're going to still need lots of plastic for furniture and concrete for buildings—and to go on having those nice things, you've got to have oil.

Having plentiful food requires oil, because fertilizer requires oil—and the global food crunch is even more implacable and unrelenting than the oil crunch. Fully one-third of the human beings living today—two billion of them—would be starving were it not for the invention of new fertilizers. Two Germans, chemist Fritz Haber and industrialist Carl Bosch, invented the Haber-Bosch process for extracting nitrates from atmospheric nitrogen just before World War I. This enabled the production of nitrate fertilizers to ensure bumper crops on a scale and quality—and affordability—previously inconceivable. For this extraordinary achievement, widely described at the time as "making bread out of air" (after all, 70 percent of the atmosphere is inert nitrogen), both men won the Nobel Prize for chemistry. (Haber's laurels were dimmed a few years later when he was the equally enthusiastic genius behind the industrial production of poison gas for use by the German army in World War I, but that's another story.)

But the Haber-Bosch process requires huge quantities of oil—and unlike electrical power–generating stations, there are no substitutes like hydrogen, coal, water, or nuclear power that can be used to do the job. Chemical equations and formulas—like mathematical ones—are unchanging and implacable. With the global population over six billion and still rising, the world needs Haber and Bosch's nitrate fertilizers—and that means it's going to go on needing oil.

This means that—until they run out—oil fields in Saudi Arabia, Kuwait, Iran, and Iraq will be even more crucial than ever. Even with the development of Nigerian and west African fields, and Russia energetically developing and selling its own huge oil and gas resources, the largest, cheapest, most easily accessible, and highest-quality petroleum reserves in the world remain in the Middle East.

Good fences make good neighbors

When Israeli prime minister Ariel Sharon started building his fence in 2002 to separate Palestinian areas of the West Bank and Gaza from Israel's heartland, most armchair strategists and pundits around the world did not think it would work. Liberals were conditioned to worry about the "root causes" of conflicts rather than the nuts and bolts of actually winning them. And many conservatives still loved the romantic idea of bold, thrilling offensive armored and blitzkrieg strikes, like those that won the 1991 and 2003 Gulf War military campaigns. Security fences along national borders and increased border controls were globally out of fashion. The Berlin Wall was torn down in 1989 by ecstatic East Germans in the nonviolent upheaval that heralded the collapse of Communism. The security fences that tore Europe in two for forty-four years collapsed as Communism crumbled.

A new era of globalism powered by worldwide economic growth and the information technology revolution followed. *New York Times* pundit Thomas Friedman heralded the arrival of a supposed "flat earth." The European Community consolidated itself into the European Union. Internal security barriers within the EU were torn down, and the customs, security, and immigration checks on its external perimeter became a joke.

But as Edward Gibbon, the great eighteenth-century English historian and author of the monumental *Decline and Fall of the Roman Empire*, could have told Friedman and the EU policymakers, a flat earth without borders was also a planet without defenses against barbarian invaders striking from every direction.

Even after September 11, most media elites in the U.S. believe the idea of a wall is too barbaric. This is a case in which the West could learn something from the Middle East.

It was tough old Sharon, always ready to push liberal buttons, who put security fences and defensible borders back on the global strategic map. Israeli hard-line right-wingers and liberal supporters of the Palestinians alike derided his concept of a security fence to cut the Gaza Strip and the Palestinian areas of the West Bank off from Israel in order to stop suicide attacks.

The fence worked. In 2003, before it was even completed, the number of terrorist attacks against Israeli civilians fell by 30 percent, and the number of civilians killed by such attacks fell by 50 percent. In the following years, the improvements continued.

Successful suicide bomber attacks fell from dozens a year to single figures. Hundreds of civilian lives per year were saved. And suddenly, serious border defenses were back in fashion.

The Indian army was so impressed by the success of the Israeli barrier that it built a similar one along the Line of Control separating Indian-controlled Jammu and Kashmir from the much smaller part of the state held by Pakistan since 1947. Soon the Indians were reporting that Islamist guerrilla incursions across the Line of Control had fallen by 80 percent. They followed up the Kashmir fence with an even longer one to surround the entire Muslim nation of Bangladesh. Bangladesh, like India, is a democracy, but Islamist extremists there have been much more active since they were driven out of Afghanistan by U.S. forces and their allies in late 2001.

The Saudis also took notice of how well Israel's fence worked. They erected one of their own to try to control their southern border with Yemen, which 400,000 illegal immigrants looking for work cross every year. They are now building one along their northeastern border with Iraq.

Sharon's fence transformed strategic calculations about how to control borders around the world. And it is a fence, not a concrete wall, contrary to much inaccurate international reporting on the subject. According to official Israeli figures, only about 6 percent, or twenty-four miles, of the four-hundred-mile fence is a thirty-foot-high concrete wall. Such barriers were erected to protect Israeli civilians from sniper fire on the other side. In one incident near Bethlehem, an eight-year-old Israeli girl was shot dead in one such attack before the wall was built. These sections look no different from the sound barriers so familiar alongside freeways and turnpikes in the United States and along motorways in Europe.

The barrier is therefore low-key and unremarkable. It is not a huge, awesome construction like an underground missile firing base. It has only a fraction of the concrete and none of the enormous heavy artillery guns that were built into the French Maginot Line or Hitler's Atlantic and Dnieper walls during World War II.

Shattering another popular myth, the barrier isn't even high-tech. None of the technologies used to build or guard it is less than sixty years old. Jeep-like patrol vehicles almost identical to the ones the U.S. Army used in World War II sweep along its dirt roads. The barbed wire it uses was invented 120 years ago. Only the movement-detection sensors are relatively sophisticated, and even there the emphasis is on toughness and reliability rather than innovation. The fence does not require any new technologies, only old-fashioned but curiously effective application of old ones.

Once the fence became fully functional in 2005, the wave of suicide bombings that killed more than a thousand Israeli civilians during the five years of the Second Intifada was stopped dead in its tracks. Since then not a single suicide bomber from either Gaza or the Palestinian Authority–controlled areas of the West Bank has been able to kill one additional Israeli civilian. In the summer and fall of 2007, the cafes along the main arteries of Tel Aviv and Jerusalem were thronged with customers day and night as though the Second Intifada had never happened. Even tourism has soared back to pre-intifada levels.

Sharon's fence—a monument to political incorrectness—was doing its job.

The Saudi solution

When Islamists detonated two bombs outside Saudi Arabian security centers at the end of December 2004, within hours three of the suspected ringleaders had been killed and others apprehended. Yet when insurgents in Iraq killed thirty government soldiers in attacks on succeeding days, they did so with impunity.

According to much American conventional wisdom at the time, neither of these things was supposed to happen. The kingdom established by old King Abdulaziz ibn Saud was supposed to be a house of cards, and the Sunni insurrection in Iraq was supposed to be a minor local difficulty. Iraq two years after the toppling of Saddam was supposed to already be a pillar of regional stability, pumping out enough oil to break the power of the OPEC cartel; Saudi Arabia was supposed to be the dangerous breeding ground for active Islamist terrorists.

Yet by the end of August 2007, more than eighteen times the number of American soldiers had been killed in Iraq since President George W. Bush declared "Mission Accomplished" on May 1, 2003, than the number of those who died during the first three weeks of occupation. And the harsh, unrelenting fact remains that the new Iraqi security forces rapidly rushed into existence to take the burden off the exhausted and undermanned U.S. forces have so far shown no ability to do the job.

Their morale is poor, their equipment miserable, and their training awful. U.S. military analysts fear the new forces are riddled with Islamist and former Ba'ath agents and that in intelligence terms they therefore leak like a sieve. In Washington, many Middle East experts now opine that the U.S. should instead have opted for building slowly and far more carefully an elite, carefully screened, and much smaller Iraqi force.

By contrast, the repeated predictions of catastrophe and doom in Saudi Arabia have been proven completely wrong. Eight years ago, with global oil prices down to a historic low of nearly ten dollars per barrel, there were indeed widespread concerns that the Saudis might be running out of cash to fund the generous and expensive social contract that has bought decades of peace and stability to the desert kingdom. But today, with global oil prices still well above eighty dollars a barrel and an energy-hungry China ravenously seeking new oil supplies from as far away as Canada and Venezuela, the Saudis certainly do not lack for financial resources to fund either their social programs or their security services.

Instead, over the past year, their revitalized security services, which were always far more effective than hostile critics in the American media often painted them, have scored one success after another against Islamist insurrectionists.

Al Qaeda's organization in Saudi Arabia has been reeling, with at least five of its leaders killed by Saudi security in only twelve months. As a result, the Saudis did more to dent the terror group's image of invincibility than four and a half years of U.S. military operations in Iraq have managed.

The most dangerous and effective enemies al Qaeda has faced have been the intelligence services of existing Arab governments, whether they be the extensive network of the Saudi monarchy, the small but highly efficient security forces of King Abdullah II in Jordan, or the Syrian intelligence service of Bashar Assad. Indeed, Syria proved to be an invaluable source of intelligence on al Qaeda in the year after the September 11 attacks.

At least for the moment, the Saudi security authorities continue to clamp down on their own militants. But in neighboring Iraq, the insurgents still have the Bush administration and their own government by the throat, not the other way around.

By contrast, a January 2005 report titled "Al Qaeda in Saudi Arabia: Asymmetric Threats and Islamist Extremists" from Washington's Center for Strategic and International Studies confirmed the Saudi success. "The al Qaeda organization in Saudi Arabia," the paper reports, "has done some damage to the kingdom's economy and has killed many innocent people." However, "this has had little impact on the day-to-day life of ordinary Saudis."

Al Qaeda has been "unsuccessful in its recruitment efforts," the report continued. "It failed to articulate a viable alternative to the existing government" and "it lacked funding and was forced to channel resources into the one existing cell—thus unable to establish other independent cells."

The report also disputed the widely held popular belief that al Qaeda is invincible because it is decentralized and can reorganize and regroup at will. This has not been the case in Saudi Arabia. "Despite the popular notion of al Qaeda as a hydra that can constantly grow new heads, there are indications that the organization has not been able to recover from government attacks. At its peak, Saudi al Qaeda claimed between 500–600 members scattered among the cells. Of these, roughly 250 were die-hards. By the end of 2004, between 400–500 militants had been captured and killed, including all of its leaders—this in addition to the thousands of its sympathizers who were arrested and interrogated, most of whom have been freed."

Once again, the paper found, border control is key. "In 2004, Saudi border guards detained nearly a million people attempting to gain illegal entry into the kingdom and captured more than ten tons of drugs (the sales of which are often used to fund guerrilla operations). In addition, there were 2,000 weapons seizures and, in all 19,000 smuggling attempts were foiled and 8,000 smugglers arrested."

Public Opinion in the Middle East

If you wonder about the future of democracy in the Middle East, check out *The Great Divide: How Westerners and Muslims View Each Other*, published in 2006 by the Pew Global Attitudes Project. Below is a sample of the data pulled from a poll of Muslims around the world:

Violence against civilian targets in order to defend Islam can be justified

Country	Often/Sometimes	Rarely	Never
Egypt	28%	25%	45%
Jordan	29%	28%	43%

Most important, however, the authors concluded, was that "the organization could not win popular support. While it was able to exploit popular feeling and anger on some issues such as the Arab-Israeli conflict, it could not win significant support for its actual activities from either Saudi people or the Saudi clergy. Above all, its emphasis on violence failed to resonate with the people. Saudis were shocked by the initial attacks, and those that targeted Muslims and Arabs further alienated and diminished support for the organization."

Nevertheless, the paper's authors cautioned against undue and premature complacency in assessing the continuing al Qaeda threat. "Saudi Arabia is at a critical juncture in its fight against terrorism. The threat is unlikely to disappear for years to come. Al Qaeda can draw on Saudis in Afghanistan, Pakistan, Yemen, and Central Asia, as well as other members of al Qaeda who may be able to enter Saudi Arabia. The Iraq and Yemeni borders present serious problems in terms of infiltration."

Ironically, while President Saddam Hussein continued to rule Iraq with a terrifyingly iron hand, the Saudis faced no threat whatsoever from al Qaeda's infiltration across that border. It was only after the U.S. occupation of Iraq and the eruption of a formidable widespread Sunni Muslim popular insurgency that this problem has exploded.

The report also noted the warning that Saudi interior minister Prince Nayef bin Abdulaziz issued at a high-level regional security meeting in Tehran: "Iraq must not be a place for training terrorists, and they could be Saudis, like what happened in Afghanistan.... The situation in Iraq endangers not only the country and its people, but it has become a clear and dangerous threat to security and stability in the region."

A safer Middle East

Americans and Europeans—and, frankly, everyone—needs to worry about the Middle East. It's not going to go away, and it's not going to leave us alone. We will need the region's oil for the foreseeable future, and even if we didn't, Israel exists, and so Arab anger will persist.

What can we do about it?

Before we can begin to develop a workable vision for peace in the Middle East, we need to slay a few politically correct dragons. First, we need to reject Michael Moore and his cronies who have decided that the Saudi regime—for the crime of being friendly with the Bush family—is the heart of all evil.

Second, we need to toss aside the feel-good idealism of Jimmy Carter and George Bush that Western-style liberal democracy can work in the region like it has in the West.

Third, we need to adjust our standards of decency, and deal with the fact that the Ottoman Empire—brutal, intolerant, and heavy-handed—worked. Also, however unpleasant the security fence may be in Israel, it's a key to peace.

If we shatter these PC idols and embrace some politically incorrect truths that history teaches us, we can start to see the path to relative peace. The key to a stable regime is not a democratic Iraq but a powerful Saudi Arabia. While the kingdom may not become an empire, it can assert its influence throughout the region. Imagine if other countries could control al Qaeda like Saudi Arabia does. The Saudis, like the Ottomans and in contrast to the British or Americans, aren't afraid to go into mosques and exert influence to quash the extremists and defend stability.

We also need to support a strong but restrained Israel. Ariel Sharon, the fierce warrior who was also pragmatic, is the model for Israeli leadership, however reviled by the Left or looked down upon by Western elites.

In all aspects of life, political correctness clouds true perception, but in the Middle East, tearing down PC myths becomes a matter of life and death for Arabs, Israelis, Europeans, and Americans.

ACKNOWLEDGMENTS

This book could not have been written without the friendship, encouragement, unflagging cheer, support, and superb professionalism of Harry Crocker, vice president of Regnery; Tim Carney, my dream editor at Regnery; and my old, dear friend John O'Sullivan, former editor-in-chief at UPI, who got the whole thing moving.

My old teacher, the late, great Professor Elie Kedourie, provided not just the fruits of his unrivaled scholarship but also his unique understanding and wisdom about a region still too much preached at and too little understood to this day. Arnaud de Borchgrave, the legendary editor and foreign correspondent, has given me the gift of his friendship as well as his astonishing sixty-plus years of experience of the region and prescient calls through all of it. It was because I worked for him for so many years at the *Washington Times* that I was able to accumulate the experience that I did.

Thanks also to Tobin Beck, Claude Salhani, Michael Marshall, Martin Walker, and Krishnadev Calamur, my longtime bosses, colleagues, and friends at UPI under whom I continued to roam and monitor the region and who made every day of covering these things a joy and a privilege.

Also to Holger Jensen and the late Woody West, who unleashed me on the region, to Wesley Pruden, Arnaud's successor as editor in chief at the *Washington Times*, and David Jones, his long-serving and much-loved foreign editor, who sent me out there so often, to Martin Hutchison, columnist on emerging markets in the *Wall Street Journal* who helped me unravel so many economic conundrums, and to Senta, for priceless advice and encouragement at exactly the right time. None of the outspoken judgments in this book should be attributed to any of them.

INDEX